THE SEVEN DEADLY SINS
(Plays)

THE SEVEN DEADLY SINS
(*Plays*)

Pierre Meunier

Spectrum Books Limited
Ibadan
Abuja • Benin City • Lagos • Owerri

Published by
Spectrum Books Limited
Spectrum House
Ring Road
PMB 5612
Ibadan, Nigeria

in association with
Safari Books (Export) Limited
1st Floor
17 Bond Street
St Helier
Jersey JE2 3NP
Channel Islands
United Kingdom.

Europe and USA Distributor
African Books Collective Ltd.
The Jam Factory
27 Park End Street
Oxford OX1, 1HU, UK

© Pierre Meunier

First published, 2001

All rights reserved. This book is copyright and so no part of it may be reproduced, stored in a retrieval system, or transmitted, in any form or by any means, electronic, mechanical, electrostatic, magnetic tape, photocopying, recording or otherwise, without the prior written permission of the copyright owner.

ISBN: 978-029-268-3

Printed by Polygraphics Venture Limited Ibadan

CONTENTS

		Page
1.	Gluttony	1
2.	Lechery or The Bet	23
3.	The Loafer	71
4.	The Cheats	99
5.	Avarice	119
6.	Envy	157
7.	Pride and Ambition or The Sun King	189

GLUTTONY

PROLOGUE

(The lady presenter arrives on the stage. Thirteen characters are lined up on the right hand side of the stage)

THE LADY PRESENTER: *(Pointing with the tip of the stick in her hand)* Here are the gentlemen who are going to personify the deadly sins. There are seven of them *(showing them one after the other)*: Pride, Avarice, Lechery, Envy, Gluttony, Anger, Laziness. It's true, but I have added six others *(she shows them too, one after the other)*: Wickedness, Discrimination, Dishonesty, Untruthfulness, Nepotism, and the last of them, quite typical of this environment, "African Time", meaning the total absence of notion of time and of respect for the time agreed for an appointment.

And here's the first of these gentlemen (*she goes towards one of the actors, holds him by the hand and pushes him before her, announcing aloud*): "GLUTTONY" (*the actor representing this sin bows down to the spectators as a mark of greetings*).

(*The curtain falls*)

ACT I

SCENE I

(*A large table is installed in the middle of the stage loaded with assorted dishes and drinks. The character representing Gluttony has an enormous roundish shape. He is sitting alone at the table and is facing the spectators. He has a red towel around his neck, his cheeks are chubby and his nose is enormous. Several servants are at attention near him, watching every gesture of his).*

He eats greedily, biting straight at the leg of mutton which he is holding in both hands. When he has finished, he throws the bone on the ground then swallows very quickly a whole plate of beans. Twenty bottles of beer are lined up in front of him, as well as bottle of whisky, cognac and gin.

Fifteen empty bottles are scattered on the ground, close to him. From time to time he belches noisily and drinks straight from the bottle of beer he has taken).

THE GLUTTON: Oh how good it is! Oh what a delicious feeling when food and drinks go down my throat! (*he snatches with the left hand a chicken leg from one of the plates and with the right, a sweet potato and continues to devour gluttonously).*

(*The curtain falls*)

SCENE II

(*An old lady, puny and small in size appears*).

THE OLD LADY: (*Counting the empty bottles and the bones scattered on the floor*) Well my friend, you were terribly hungry and thirsty! Seventeen bottles of beer already swallowed. Two legs of mutton, three chickens, four plates of potatoes, three plates of beans devoured by you alone! Yes, you must have been terribly hungry and your appetite is wonderful!

THE GLUTTON: (*Interrupting her*) Keep quiet mother, you get on my nerves with your refrain which is always the same! You eat too much! You drink too much! You eat too much, you drink too much! Always the same old chorus, when in fact I'm trying to control this insatiable appetite, which I'm lucky to have! Look at yourself. You are as dry as a rake; your weight, clothes included, is only 35 kilos!

THE OLD LADY: But my son, it is for your own good that I say this to you, you are my only son and I prefer to see you alive than dead!

THE GLUTTON: Look old goat! Stop preaching! You hear? My greatest pleasure in life is to eat well and to drink well! So to die fat or skinny... one has to die, no? In any case if I became lean I think I would die immediately. So mother, do you want to see me dead? Is that what you want? Tell me!

THE OLD LADY: (*To herself*) There's nothing I can do, I better not waste my breath... he will die with his huge paunch, this big pot belly which he drags along like a millstone round his waist! One digs his tomb with his teeth they say. Well, my son has already dug his tomb, there, near him, half ready, yawning with boredom and impatiently waiting to take custody of his dead body! (*aloud*) Well, my son, I'm leaving you to your feast, worthy of Lucullus, but don't come and weep in my lap when it's too late!

THE GLUTTON: (*A leg of chicken in his mouth*) Shut up, old bag! Leave me to eat in peace and long live Lucullus, Pantagruel, and Gargantua! (*devouring the leg of chicken*) Not to mention Gargamel,

	their worthy mother and wife. (*Throwing the bone in the direction of his mother*). Go away you old witch! Clear off! Away! Beat it!
THE OLD LADY:	(*Aloud*) I'm off you fatty! My fat little son! Grow as fat as you can. And take the size and weight you want. You will see when you die! (*aside*) Oh my God! The doctor has just arrived. I know him, there is no mistake possible. I hope he'll be luckier than me and will convince this pig-headed son of mine that his life is in danger (*she goes out*).

(*The curtain falls*)

SCENE III

DOCTOR: (*Entering with his attache case and stethoscope around his neck*) Good day all!

THE GLUTTON: (*Grumbling between two mouthfuls*) What is it again? Who is this intruder, this undesirable person coming to disturb my feast? (*taking a gulp of beer straight from the bottle and looking in the direction of the doctor*) Ah, is it you doctor?

DOCTOR: Yes, it's me. I have come to see how you are getting on.

THE GLUTTON: How I'm getting on?

DOCTOR: Yes, how you are getting on: stomach, liver, spleen, heart, and all the rest!

THE GLUTTON: Stomach, liver, spleen, heart, but all those things are working perfectly. I eat for four and digest for six!

DOCTOR: Let us see your weight, first! Get on the scale which is under the table.

THE GLUTTON: Again your torture of the scale! It's worse than Chinese torture, that thing! Besides, it is very indiscreet. Moreover, first of all I must get it out. (*Coming on his knees to get it out*) Oh how difficult it is! (*falling flat on the floor*) Good God, what's happening to me?

DOCTOR: (*Roaring with laughter*) Too much fatness leads you...

THE GLUTTON: Help, doctor! I'm dying! I'm suffocating

DOCTOR: And a disastrous overweight!

THE GLUTTON: Have mercy, doctor, help me!

DOCTOR: You have too many kilos, my little friend. I should rather say my big, my fat friend. Yes too many superfluous kilos. Your organs are drowned in fat; the heart, the liver, the spleen, in short, everything.

THE GLUTTON: Have mercy, doctor, I'm going to die! (*He begins to weep*).

DOCTOR: First promise me that you will eat less, then I will help you.

THE GLUTTON:	I do promise, doctor, I am going to put myself on a starvation diet, and will fast once a week ...
DOCTOR:	Do you promise?
THE GLUTTON:	Yes, doctor. Certainly ...
DOCTOR:	Really promise?
THE GLUTTON:	I swear to God, doctor, I swear on my own head!
DOCTOR:	(*Aside*) It's meaningless to swear on a head like his, a head that could drop any day, any time (*talking to the glutton*). Right, I'm going to help you (*going near him*). Now, a little effort (*making him turn*). Lie on your back (*helping him to sit*). Now sit in an upright position (*helping him to get up, amidst laughter*). And take the normal position of the biped you are.
THE GLUTTON:	Thank you, doctor. Without you I would have been dead.
DOCTOR:	Oh I didn't do much.
THE GLUTTON:	And buried!
DOCTOR:	And now my dear, get on to the scale!

THE GLUTTON: (*Stepping to the scale and finding it difficult to keep his balance*) It's moving, doctor. It's oscillating. It's shaking under my feet.

DOCTOR: (*Watching where the arrow stops*) Good heavens! You now weigh more than the scale can record! Come down quickly before you break it! All the same, more than 130 kilos in one man, it is unbelievable!

THE GLUTTON: So what are we going to do?

DOCTOR: It's very easy. I'm going to bring the scale which I have in my car. You will put one foot on this one and another on mine (*he goes out*).

THE GLUTTON: Fine, doctor.

DOCTOR: (*Returning with his scale under his armpit*) Here's the machine. I am putting it close to the other one, and you are going to put, as I said, a foot on one, a foot on the other. Come on, do it!

THE GLUTTON: (*Moving slowly to the two scales*) Here's it, a foot here, a foot there. (*Having great difficulties to keep his balance*) Quick, doctor! Otherwise I'm going to fall. Quick!

DOCTOR:	(*Adjusting his spectacles*) A bit of patience. Hold on! That's it! One says 74, the other reads 72. The total is ... (*calculating*) You may now get down. The total is 146 kilos. Now let me do a medical check-up of this huge mass of yours. First of all let me measure your size (*he takes out a graduated ribbon and measures the perimetre of the glutton*). Good God! Hell! Incredible! It's incredible. No more, no less! Exactly two metres! I just managed to take your measurements (*going around the enormous body of the glutton and applying his stethoscope to different parts of the body and even to places not usually examined by medical doctor*). Incredible! It's incredible.
THE GLUTTON:	What is so incredible?
DOCTOR:	That you are still alive, my friend. No more, no less. Your body is blocked with fat, just like the sea in the north or south pole is blocked with ice. A living ice bank that's what you are my dear fellow, and if you don't make all this melt, it's death! I guarantee you!
THE GLUTTON:	Death, doctor?

DOCTOR: Death!

THE GLUTTON: Death? If it is so I'm going to make all that melt, doctor, I swear!

DOCTOR: Goodbye, sir. And let me know when a single scale is enough to record your weight (*he goes away after having collected his scale*).

THE GLUTTON: Goodbye, doctor... I will call you very soon, you can be sure (*to himself*). Yes, I'm going to melt. I swear! No more ice bank, no more north pole, no more south pole! (*taking his guard, his two fists in front*) and the excess kilos should better behave themselves! (*pretending to be boxing*) On guard you blackguards!

(*The curtain falls*)

SCENE IV

The Glutton is seated before the same table, loaded with more food and bottles than even before.

THE GLUTTON: (*Talking to himself*) If something has melted, it's my good resolutions which have disappeared like snow in the sun and not the "ice bank", not the excess kilos. I eat more than ever. I'm swelling before my very eyes and soon I will need three or four scales to take my weight! (*his teeth biting a pineapple*) Greed, gluttony is my greatest weakness, I know. It's one of the deadly sins, I know. But what I don't know is how to get rid of this plague! When I see good things on a table, my eyes lit up, my nostrils palpitate, my tongue quakes, my mouth waters and my stomach laughs or weeps! (*he gulps a bottle of beer, then another, followed by another, and falls flat asleep on the table. He snores noisily*).

(*Then comes his wife*).

THE WIFE:	(*Going nearer to him*) (*aside*) My useless husband is here again sleeping. In any case what else does he do apart from sleeping, eating and drinking? Drinking, eating, sleeping ... These are the only three things that preoccupy him. Sleeping, drinking, eating,... going from bed to table and from table to bed! Is that a husband? You must be joking! It's been ages since he sleeps with me and instead of murmuring sweet nothing to me, ages those heavy snores take the place of words of love, and those lips and tongue are only used to taste food and drinks, instead of giving me sweet kisses and shivers!
THE GLUTTON:	(*Snoring more than ever*) Rrrrr... rrr...
THE WIFE:	Oh the boor! The vile creature! To snore like this when he should be warming up my love! (*she takes a stick and gets ready to strike him but changes her mind*).
THE GLUTTON:	(*Ceases to snore and dream*) Where am I? Am I dreaming or are all these marvellous things I see on the table real? (*admiring*) Good God! What a pleasant aroma! This is coming from the big cooking pot over

	there. Let's see. A jugged hare, my God. It's my favourite dish!
THE WIFE:	(*Raising her stick*) He's going to see if it's a dream, (*striking him*) or reality!
THE GLUTTON:	(*Raising his arms in self-defence*). Which devil is beating me? It's no longer a dream, this time, but a nightmare! These are strokes of a stick. By God! And real ones at that! What beats me all is that, they are being delivered by my dear wife! Behind me enraged bitch! Behind me wretched creature!
THE WIFE:	Take this! Have a few more strokes lazy fool, loafer! That will help put your ideas straight and put your feet back on earth! Good-for-nothing! Windbags! Take this for the mad bitch (*she strikes him*). And this for the wretched creature! (*she strikes him again*).
THE GLUTTON:	(*Groaning*) Stop you wicked woman! You are taking advantage that the stick is in your hand. But you won't get off lightly when I get hold of you!
THE WIFE:	Have this one too (*striking him again*). It won't cost you any more, my little

fellow! One more or one less!

THE GLUTTON: (*Seizing the stick*) Now it's my turn to act, you devilish creature (*he tries to hit her, but she dodges and moves again*).

THE WIFE: (*Bursting into laughter*) Hey fatty, run! My God, stretch your legs and catch me if you can!

THE GLUTTON: (*Who cannot run*) Devil, scoundrel! I divorce you! I divorce you! I divorce you! (*throwing the stick at her*) Go away. You are no longer my wife!

THE WIFE: I'm off and very happy to leave such a husband. You, a husband? No! A snorer? Yes! You a husband? No! A wine bag, a soak? Yes! You a husband? No! A demi-john? Yes! I too divorce you, I divorce you, I divorce you and I'm going away as free as a bird (*she dances a few steps and goes away humming*).

THE GLUTTON: (*Following her with his eyes*) Ah at last I have got rid of a burden. Now I'll be able to eat whatever I want (*looking at the dishes spread on the table*). And as much as I want, (*moving towards the table*) drink to my fill, and snore at ease (*he settles down at the large table*

	and begins to eat. Then comes a visitor carrying a parcel).
THE VISITOR:	(*Comes close to him*) Sir, sir, (*signalling with the hand).* I have something for you.
THE GLUTTON:	(*Groaning*) What! Another idiot coming to disturb me!
THE VISITOR:	A huge sum of money that you have won.
THE GLUTTON:	(*His mouth full)* Each thing in its own time!
THE VISITOR:	₦50,000 here in the parcel all in brand new Murtala!
THE GLUTTON:	Thanks. Drop the parcel there (*pointing to a table*). I'm at this very moment very busy filling my stomach and I have no time for buying and selling (*continuing to devour greedily).* Goodbye my friend and know that tomorrow is another day!
THE VISITOR:	(*Going away, pensive and doubtful*). (*Aloud*) Goodbye sir, it's better if I come back (*aside*) I never saw such a glutton, whose stomach matters more than money! (*then comes a very pretty*

young lady, wearing a miniskirt and as enticing as one can dream. She gets near the glutton while wriggling her bottom).

THE GLUTTON: (*Glancing absent-mindedly and continuing to swallow food*) What's the object of your visit?

THE LADY: (*Moving so close as to brush against him*) From far off, I saw you all alone, very lonesome, so I thought that as I'm alone too, and lonesome, we could end our solitude and enjoy ourselves together.

THE GLUTTON: (*Pushing her brutally and howling*). Each thing in its own time, ok? (*Making horrible grimaces*). So there is time for the leg of turkey which I'm right now devouring, and time for your legs which to me appear to be hospitable! (*changing his mind and running his left hand on her buttocks, while, with the right he continues to eat. The girl kisses him*). It's true that you're quite pretty and plump in all parts of your body and I would be mad to ignore such treasures. But you'll have to wait, sweetie... Let's eat first! Here you are. Take whatever you like – chicken, guinea fowl, venison, mutton, and you can drink till your

	thirst is quenched and till you lose your head, the best beverages this house can offer.
THE LADY:	I'm straightaway going to nibble at venison which I do not know yet (*she kisses him on the cheeks tenderly, with a click of the lips*).
THE GLUTTON:	(*Embracing her with the left arm and caressing the left breast he is holding in his hand*).

> I am greedy, it's clear.
> And I like the good things of life
> And everyone of them!
> Therefore let's imitate Lucullus,
> And after sacrifice to Venus,
> To forget our woes!

THE LADY: My lord let's join our lives, beauty, joy, charms will calm your desires. You agree, don't you?

THE GLUTTON: (*Kissing her neck*).
I agree, my dear,
My sweety dear,
And I will follow you
My turtle-dove.
(*Kissing her this time on the lips*).
I agree,
My dove

And I'm flying
Swiftly away.
Yes, with you,
It goes without saying,
To sing and laugh
with you.
(*Both continue to eat, tenderly hugged*).

THE GLUTTON:	Ah to die while eating and caressing you! That would be, as far as I'm concerned, the most beautiful way to die. Ah to die with the mouth full of delicious flesh and good wine! (*Raising a bottle of wine above his head*). Like this one for instance. So what do you say to that, sweety?

THE LADY:	That's my wish too.
The dearest of them all.
Without the slightest doubt.

THE GLUTTON:	You are the bird that sings
and cheers the nest
I'm the bird which boasts
that it can provide everything.

(*The curtain falls*).

SCENE V

THE LADY PRESENTER: (*The Lady presenter, alone on the stage*). So you have seen the first of these gentlemen (*pointing at the Glutton who reappears and greets*). Greed! Gluttony! Believe me, is a very ugly sin which makes you ugly and fat, and lures you away from the right path.
(*She chases him away, pretending to beat him with a stick*).

THE GLUTTON: (*Fleeing and shouting*) No! No! No sticks on my back. I'm leaving without waiting to hear more!

(*The curtain falls*)

LECHERY OR THE BET

CAST:

THE LADY PRESENTER:)
THE GLUTTON:) Characters in the prologue
THE LECHER:)
THEOPHILUS JOHNSON (Theo) The apprentice Lecher

AMADEUS DA SILVA (Amy): The "professor" of lechery
ANGELA: One of the hired call girls
GLORIA: Amadeus's mistress.
CLEO: Theo's girlfriend.
ZACHARIA: The originator of the bet.

PROLOGUE:

The lady presenter arrives on the stage. Thirteen dummies are lined up on the right-hand side of the stage. Two of them are real persons representing greed and lechery. Their respective sins are written boldly on their chests.

THE LADY PRESENTER: (*Points to the person representing greed with the tip of the stick in her hand*). You see this sorrowful gentleman representing gluttony (*she touches him with her stick*). He's a miserable creature indeed, huge, fat, and frightfully ugly.

	You may now leave, Mr Glutton (*she hits him with her stick*). Away! We've seen enough of your abominable round shape. Move! (*She chases him in front of her*) At a trot! At the double!
THE GLUTTON:	(*Crying as he runs away*) No! Have pity for goodness sake! Don't hit my back, I'm leaving, asking for nothing more.
THE LADY PRESENTER:	Oh my God! We've seen enough of that one. Let's see the second one of these (*she moves towards the actor representing Lechery, holds him by the hand and pushes him before her, announcing in a loud voice*) Ladies and gentlemen, here comes Mr Lecher.
THE LECHER:	(*Bowing low to the audience*) Ladies and gentlemen; Lechery! Here I am!

(*The curtain falls*)

ACT I

SCENE I

The action takes place in a large hall, opening on the outside by a large door. On either side of the hall are three doors, and a much larger door far off. The walls are covered with enlarged pictures of pretty young ladies. A huge one presents a young man with fine pleasant features.

JOHNSON: (*Entering the empty room and looking at the pictures*) Oh my God! But there's nobody, not a cat, not a soul! (*seeing the three doors on the left and the three on the right*). Let me knock at one of these doors and see. Nothing wrong in that (*he knocks timidly at first, then as no reply is forthcoming, violently*).

WOMAN'S VOICE FROM
BEHIND THE DOOR: Yes, darling, come in, I'm waiting for you...

JOHNSON: (*Moving backwards*) Good God, what does that mean?

THE WOMAN:	(*Opening the door*) So Amy are you coming? I'm ready to satisfy all your needs!
JOHNSON:	(*Stunned*) Have I ... have I come to the right address?
THE WOMAN:	(*Appearing on the steps of the door in a see-through neligee*) Yes, my dear... (*seeing the visitor*). Oh! Excuse me sir (*closing the door*).
JOHNSON:	(*Going to the next door*) Let me try that one. I may be luckier to run into the owner of the house (*knocking hard*). Let's see...
A WOMAN'S VOICE:	Just a minute darling, and I'll be yours, all yours!
JOHNSON:	Good Heavens! I'm on the wrong track again, misled, lost (*he tries the third door. The same dialogue and the same comic game occurs, gathering momentum at the fourth, fifth and sixth doors*). Good God! But this is the den of blue beard! What? The body of a woman quite alive no doubt, behind each door! They must have been making fun of me and pulling my legs when they said to me: 'Go to Creek village, there you'll

have the encounter of your life! Amadeus Da Silva, the most virtuous person on the entire coast will amaze you! Well, seeing all the sweet little faces behind each of the six doors I knocked at, the gentleman called Amadeus Da Silva must have his own peculiar kind of virtue!

(*Walking up and down, his hands crossed behind his back*) But, patience. Let's wait till the host arrives and we shall see what kind of a bird he is (*stopping at one of the six doors, and combing his hair*). Now, a little combing and a tightening of the necktie-knot. (*Making comic gestures describing the contours of a woman, breasts and buttocks, and indicating that with a bit of courage he would be willing to enter*) (*low*). If I were more daring I would go in. It's behind this door that I should be waiting. That's where the most beautiful of them all is nestling. Let's see. Which of the doors is it? The third on the left? Yes that's it. Third on the left. In any case the door is numbered. Wonderful! And it's number 6! A number I mustn't forget. Nobody knows, one day, perhaps, or one night, eh, one very dark moonless night, I may come back here stealthily without being seen, and... (*aloud*). To hell with all these lecherous ideas invading my head. Let me leave this place. These walls are haunted by the devil and this Da Silva chap seems to me to be none other than the devil's advocate (*making a gesture as if driving somebody away*). Vade Retro Satana! (*in a low tone*). But never in my life did I see such pretty eyes. The low neckline of the dress led me to imagine the existence of divine treasures indeed, and such carnal treasures must end up in divine pleasures... My God, why do you constantly put such insidious temptations on my way. These wolf-traps from which one has the utmost difficulty to escape. (*Aloud*) Is there anybody in this den, this lair, apart from these fairies dropped from heaven or hell?

SCENE II

(*The farthest door opens and there emerges the man whose photo is hanging on the wall*)

DA SILVA: (*Soliloquizing*) I wonder when the man from Maiduguri of whom I have heard so much about is coming. The stage is superbly set. Everything looks so natural that he's going to fall into the trap without realising anything. All the same, let me take a glance at the whole thing and let me find out if these chicks on my pay list have learned their parts properly (*noticing the visitor*) (*low tone*). O my, here's the man I have been expecting. Yes indeed! Small, bespectacled, plump, prematurely bald, the exact picture of a bookworm from a university! But let me go near. (*Talking to the visitor*) Hello, good morning sir. To whom do I have the honour of speaking?

JOHNSON: (*Aloud*) Oh sir, to a humble traveller who is very happy to meet you (*low*). But is it for meeting the virtuous man I have heard so much·about or the blue beard or Don Juan he apparently is?

DA SILVA: I am happy to meet you and to welcome you into my house. My name is Amadeus Da Silva, I am in business, in all kinds of deals – commercial, politico-commercial, industrial etc. Take note by the way that I am (*bursting into laughter*) something of a swindler, an expert in sentimental affairs, etc. A business man without the slightest doubt. Running a prosperous business and having a street named after him. But note also that I am above all a specialist in sentimental affairs. In that field, I am a chief! More than a knight! A king! How stupid of me to have chosen the lowest possible title in nobility! I am a Count, a Duke or even a Prince! What about you, dear sir?

JOHNSON: I have no street, no lane, not even a footpath named after me! I am just an ordinary professor teaching philosophy of all subjects, and in a modest university in Maiduguri.

DA SILVA: (*Pretending not to know the name*) Maiduguri? It's the first time in my life I hear such a name. Maiduguri! Maiduguri! The name sounds pleasant to the ear. What about your name sir?

JOHNSON: A very modest name that tinkles like a cracked bell when it falls! Johnson Theophilus. Johnson, the son of John.

DA SILVA: (*Aloud*) Well, Mr Johnson, to what do I owe the honour of your visit? (*low*) I know it too well. It would be a pleasure to have fun at the expense of this solemn academic. It all started a couple of months ago in Maiduguri, a town I know very well as I visit it twice or thrice a year. During a very boozy party where whisky, beer, gin and wine were flowing freely, a university lecturer, a jovial fellow, mentioned his name as one showing no interest in the fair sex. Fairly tipsy, I swore to turn his head to such an extent that he would forget about philosophy, religion, morality, and devote his life to Venus. A fellow, who must have been very rich and who must have known Johnson very well, bet ₦50,000 that I could not. I accepted the bet and I'm still wondering what devil pushed me to do it. Anyhow, ₦50,000 is at stake and there's no going back!

JOHNSON: Ah Mr Da Silva, I'm on holiday. After one has spent years in Maiduguri in the torrid heat of the semi-desert, I wished to know something else, something very different. According to some friends of mine, Creek town and Maiduguri are poles apart in terms of vegetation and climate.

DA SILVA: Fine. I now understand why you are in the Creek town but why did you come to my place in particular?

JOHNSON: For a simple reason. Many friends of mine who apparently know you well advised me to come and see you if I came to Creek town. Well here I am, in Creek town, right before you. And I've come to greet you.

DA SILVA: And what did they say about me, these friends of yours claiming to know me so well? Terrible things, I am sure!

JOHNSON: Far from it, Mr Da Silva. They see you as the most virtuous man of the west-coast! That's why I am here!

DA SILVA: (*Bursting out laughing*) Me, the most virtuous man of the west coast? But why not of the entire earth? And of other planets? Your so-called friends have deceived you! My dear Johnson, I'm a plain pleasure seeker, a horrible one at that, having all the vices and very few virtues if any.

JOHNSON: (*Looking scared*) Mr Da Silva... You are surely exaggerating, a man like you?

DA SILVA: I remain a pleasure seeker wallowing in lechery, enjoying it, and making no attempt to hide it. I leave to hypocrites and tartuffes the trouble of concealing their dissolute conduct behind an innocent and prudish appearance!

JOHNSON: (*Making the sign of the cross*) I can't believe my eyes, or rather my ears!

DA SILVA: So you are on holiday. Well... Well dear professor! I invite you to be my guest all through your holidays. You'll see the kind of life I lead. You'll teach me philosophy while I show you another way of life.

JOHNSON: I accept your kind invitation, but...

DA SILVA: But... Always a "but"... but. Have you so many ties restricting your movements? Are you married, or engaged to somebody? Or are you a mere priest?

JOHNSON: I am neither married nor engaged. And I am not a priest either.

DA SILVA: Have you taken a vow of abstinence?

JOHNSON: Not at all.

DA SILVA: Then what has that "but" to do here?

JOHNSON: Well... Philosophy determines my line of conduct.

DA SILVA: Philosophy? What kind of philosophy is it that determines your line of conduct?

JOHNSON: It is a philosophy that keeps me away from temptation, and from fornication.

DA SILVA:	You should throw overboard a philosophy so down to earth. What! Proscribing romance? Why aren't you married?
JOHNSON:	I could jolly well be. But my philosophy forbids fornication!
DA SILVA:	Eh! Eh! Eh! All forms of fornication? To hell with that! Forget that jumble. Be strong and undaunted! Take a complete holiday, my dear. Forget about everything – lectures, students, university and your blasted philosophy!
JOHNSON:	My good resolutions are beginning to melt like snow in the sun or like butter in the frying pan.
DA SILVA:	They will melt even more rapidly after you have seen what you are going to see! Follow me! (*going towards the first of the doors which are to his right*) That's the room of Angela, an angel fallen from heaven. She's as beautiful as daylight, as sweet as an evening in spring. Get ready, my dear, for the delicious shock that's going to dazzle you!
JOHNSON:	I'm all ready, my friend, all ears, and my eyes are wide open... and my other senses stimulated in the extreme.

DA SILVA: I'll henceforth call you Theophilus or Theo, it's more friendly. You call me Amadeus or Amy. Agreed?

JOHNSON: Okay, Amy!

DA SILVA: Well, Theo, have your senses been stimulated or not? Angela is going to disturb them and turn your wise head upside down!

JOHNSON: Amy I'm ready. For better or worse.

SCENE III

DA SILVA: (*Knocking at the door*) Peek-a-boo Angela, it's me!

ANGELA: (*Through the door*) Is it you my darling? Is it you my love? Not that scatterbrain who knocked at my door, disturbed my peace of mind and slunk away on seeing me scantily dressed, gaping as if confronted by the devil himself.

JOHNSON: (*Aside*) Scatterbrain? Me? I have fallen very low in her estimation. The young maiden was virtually naked, her breasts aimed at me... All the same, to call me a scatterbrain.

DA SILVA: The scatterbrain is here, Angela. Open, so that I introduce him to you.

ANGELA: (*Unlocking the door*) Come my darling... I am all yours, body and soul!

DA SILVA: Let's go in!

JOHNSON: (*Excited and nervous like a schoolboy*) Oh yes Amy. Let's enter... Let's enter...

ANGELA: (*Appearing on the threshold, scantily clad, rushes to throw her arms around Da*

	Silva's neck) Oh my darling (*kissing him on the lips)*. You have been away for so long that I have begun to languish. But the simple fact is that you are now present and I am bucked up!
DA SILVA:	Angela, my pet, this time we are two. Your "Scatterbrain" is here, having eyes only for you! Now he is ripe and ready to rub shoulders and other parts of his body with the high society that all of you form, my sweet darlings! Nothing can stop him! Am I right, professor?
JOHNSON:	I cannot say yet... Amy! I am still hesitant. My mind is still hazy, muddled, confused by what remains of my philosophy.
ANGELA:	I shall be a good fairy to you and help you get rid of your fears. One kiss of mine is worth ten magic wands (*going nearer Johnson to kiss him*).
JOHNSON:	(*Raising his arms as if to protect himself*) Tomorrow perhaps, beautiful Hetaira... but...
DA SILVA:	Still your "but". When will you stop being hedged in by your buts.
JOHNSON:	But...

DA SILVA: Theo, what a lout you are! Make the first move man and stop despising the feminine charms within your reach! Get to know each other, you two. I'll be back in a couple of hours (*closing the door behind them*). When the two of you are on first name terms let me know (*alone and opening the door of the next room*). Let me say hello to Maggie (*opening a second door*) and hello to Tina... and may this day be a festive day!

(*The curtain falls*)

SCENE IV

JOHNSON: (*Coming out completely dishevelled, with traces of lipstick all over the face*) Am I too a pleasure seeker? A poor bastard wallowing in lechery? Four solid hours and two minutes, by my own watch – spent, yes spent in the real sense of the word – in this den of iniquity, having completely forgotten God and all the saints. To think that I came to Creek town to spend my holidays quietly. To rub shoulders with a man reputed for his virtues. To enjoy the green vegetation and the water so much in abundance here. To enjoy the sweet and cool air after so many years of sand, drought and hell! As to enjoyment and pleasure, I have found them, though in a completely different form, more sensual than anything else. And I don't know whether I've been in hell or in heaven! And whether the creature I was kissing a short while ago is an angel or a devil, a woman in the flesh or a houri! (*talking to Angela who has remained in the room*) Sweet lady, tell me, what's your name? Is it Angela, angel? Or Demona, demon?

ANGELA: (*Bursting out laughing*) Theo... darling!

JOHNSON: Now let's see. Where's my host? Into which room did he retire and into whose arms has he fallen?

DA SILVA: (*Coming in*) Ah professor... What has become of your philosophy?

JOHNSON: My philosophy? Flattened! Out of shape! Kaput! Dead! Annihilated! I am swimming in debauchery, wallowing in lust!

DA SILVA: I told you Angela was going to disrupt your sense and put your head in a whirl?

JOHNSON: It has been done and well done. The most terrible part of the affair is that I enjoy being in that mire and that I want to wallow in it!

DA SILVA: Congratulations, my dear. You've only seen Angela. How would you feel after having seen Maggie, Tina and Gloria?

JOHNSON: Oh Gloria! You're the most beautiful of creatures. I'll see you tomorrow, unfailingly!

DA SILVA: Oh no! No way! Tomorrow is the turn of Nina, my dear Theo. There must be order in disorder, you know!

JOHNSON: Order in disorder. I like that, it sounds very well and it means what it says. As for disorder, I'm neck-deep in it (*in a plaintive tone*). I love you, Gloria.

DA SILVA: Man don't let your tongue hang out like that! She'll soon be yours.

JOHNSON: I'm pleased to hear that! But there's one thing I'd like to know.

DA SILVA: Name it!

JOHNSON: How do you manage to fill your numerous rooms with such excellent stuff.

DA SILVA: Eleven. Six opening onto the hall, five on to the garden at the back.

JOHNSON: To fill eleven rooms with such equally pretty creatures?

DA SILVA: It's not difficult. You have to be organised, that's all. As the months go by I improve and refine my methods.

JOHNSON: (*Showing a great interest*) Which methods, Amy? Tell me!

DA SILVA: Theo! How curious you are and how interested all of a sudden! Once back in Maiduguri do you intend to put my methods into practice?

JOHNSON: Me? (*stammering*) Me? How... How could you think of that, Amy?

DA SILVA: Well! It's very simple! I have touts, procurers of sorts, who comb the countryside and the towns in search of rare birds. Then there are those enticing adverts that easily catch the eyes and the minds of these young ladies, as the fish is enticed by the bait. Then there's my personal action which is far from negligible as I operate in the universities.

JOHNSON: The universities?

DA SILVA: Yes, the universities and colleges. I have great power of seduction. The eleven rooms are always occupied. These young ladies remain here for as long as they wish. They are as free as birds. The only thing that makes them stay is love, physical love as well as other kinds of love, more profound and subtle. My home is neither a prison nor a brothel, God forbid! It could be a seraglio with its harem, but a free harem without eunuchs or guards. I'm the only man to woo these ladies and if I have made an exception for you, it's because I am magnanimous. You are in my good books, believe me. It's a privilege that I am granting you to enjoy the favours of the Maggies, Ninas and, of course, Angela.

JOHNSON: But you are a... (*unable to find the word*).

DA SILVA: Again your "buts", Theo? It's the virgins who are at a premium in my quest for love, for I derive immense pleasure in initiating and conditioning! I'm the high priest of love, Theo! And these young "vestals" keep my ardour ablaze. As to love games and jousts, I am all fire and flame!

JOHNSON: A high-priest of love you really are, Amy. I appreciate the generosity of the prince of this peculiar church for accepting me in his seraglio.

DA SILVA: Theo, my motto is *primum amare deinde philosophari,* love before philosophy, but yours is perhaps the opposite.

JOHNSON: It isn't any longer, dear Amy!

DA SILVA: But I have changed it to suit my taste and now it is physical love before philosophy. *Primum fornicare deinde philosophari.*

JOHNSON: It is much better this way, my good Prince, my high-priest, at least for the time I am to spend here. By the way what is today? (*Consulting the calendar*) Ah! Thursday, the third. So I still have eighteen days' holidays. The 10th of July, and then bye-bye carnal pleasures, hello philosophy!

DA SILVA: We'll see to it Theo. First, we're going to have some refreshments and sleep like logs. Then we shall go and court our sweet ladies. I'll go to Florence, you to Nina.

JOHNSON: What a treat! I never had such a fine time! Bye Angela. Hallo Nina, what a lively life, Amy! I'd like my holidays to last for ever! Long live lust! The most enjoyable of all the deadly sins which I'm not going to part with soon.

(*The curtain falls*)

SCENE V

(*An enormous calendar shows that it is the 10th of July*).

DA SILVA: (*Alone*) Have I won the bet? 50,000 naira is at stake. The little professor has really changed. He's now devoted to Venus, undeniably! I've won and the "packet" is already mine! But I am after a total and clear victory. For that reason let's see what he's going to do next (*he goes out by the back door*).

JOHNSON: (*Comes in and looks at the calendar*) Already the 10th, and I'm yet to brush against the body of Gloria, Room 8. Such a body deserves a deep and thorough exploration. I must spend another two, three, no, four weeks! To develop my human relations, I must... remain. It is imperative! Amy will find an understanding quack to sell me a fake medical certificate and give me two months of convalescence. Amy and I are now the very best of friends. We are on first name terms!

DA SILVA: (*Comes in*) So brother, are you looking at the calendar? I overheard what you said. You have nothing to worry about. I can find ten, twenty, thirty quacks,

	ready to swear that you are at the point of death! So have no fear about your certificate my lad! It's in the bag!
JOHNSON:	Yes I was looking at this day with anguish but what you tell me gives me joy. Four weeks of grace would be welcome indeed! Gloria is mine for a first, second, third round and the finale!
DA SILVA:	You love Gloria that much? I recommend you room eleven. A new girl has just arrived, a fresh blown flower ready to learn by heart whatever she's taught. What about her, mate?
JOHNSON:	I'm scared of being a bad teacher in that kind of philosophy, having so much more to learn than teach.
DA SILVA:	Innovate, my dear. Give free rein to your fantasy, to your phantasms!
JOHNSON:	Oh treasured lechery by which I'm chained, how sweet are your ties! I would like to remain your captive for ever. So Amy, you recommend room number 11?
DA SILVA:	Yes, number 11 where Cleo reigns. That's her name.
JOHNSON:	Cleo... Cleo... Cleopatra... If she's as beautiful as her famous namesake!

DA SILVA: More beautiful, and alive! And what an energy! A force of nature, a new-born volcano of passion.

JOHNSON: A volcano? Amy, did you say a volcano? My God! Indeed, a volcano! Then I must rush there immediately! I know all about flames, and fires. I am the opposite of a pyromaniac, for instead of lighting, I put out fires! (*going out shouting*) A volcano... A volcano... Room number 11.

DA SILVA: (*Aside*) Well, lust has got the better part of him. He is caught in it neck-deep. To get out, he will need lots and lots of philosophy! I can well imagine a hand-to-hand fight between philosophy and lust. It's no use to say that the latter will win! Men have more inclination towards the baser instincts than towards the nobler ones! So I have won the bet, and the 50,000 naira is practically in my pocket! Besides, I can be proud of myself for having won this professor over to the cause of lechery and made of a sage lover and slave of the flesh. I've won my bet hands down! He can now go back to Maiduguri and proclaim having met the most virtuous man of the whole coast (*going towards room No. 8*). Let me go and say hellow to Gloria, my favourite, my true companion, whose heart is entirely mine and not for the professor!

SCENE VI

GLORIA: (*Emerging from her room*) Amy darling I was getting ready to go out for a breath of fresh air and stretch my legs a bit. Ah Amy, one thing. For goodness sake, don't let this Theo come to disturb me. The more I forbid him to take liberties with me, the more he comes back pestering me. You can imagine the sort of liberties I mean! He quite simply demands vile postures, too shameful to mention. He claims that it's you who have told him to invent, innovate, give free rein to his fantasy and to his phantasms.

DA SILVA: Indeed I did. But there are fantasies and there are fantasies, phantasms and phantasms. How could I foresee that a professor of philosophy slip so far into lechery.

GLORIA: That's where you are wrong, Amadeus. Lechery held in check and repressed for long explodes one day and then nothing can stop it!

DA SILVA: Shed your fears. I have connected him with Cleo, the newly arrived girl. She's *vesuvius,* that girl, *Etna, stromboli!* She will in no time extinguish his flame,

	believe me, and put him on his knees, turning the tiger in him into a doggie!
GLORIA:	Tiger or doggie, I don't want him on my knees, on my bed, or on my lips! That dirty pig!
DA SILVA:	Be nice and understanding, Gloria. In love, the poor chap is months, nay years, behind! He wants to make up for it in a single day! Cool down, darling. Cleo will make her room a kennel for that guy!
GLORIA:	I hope you are right!
DA SILVA:	Trust me, I'll see to it. Gloria, quick, let's go at once and forget about this boor! (*Both of them enter Room No. 8 while Johnson comes out of number 11*).

SCENE VII

JOHNSON: (*Followed by the beautiful Cleo*). (*Undertone*) Cleo is worth a hundred Glorias. Room number eleven has superceded number eight (*aloud*). Oh Cleo, my little *Vesusvius, my stromboli and my Etna.* You make me feel truly great! (*hugging her*) I love you Cleo. For your sake I'm ready to abandon my professorial chair. O Cleo, my Venus in the flesh, I devote myself entirely to the worship of your beautiful body!

CLEO: You can really talk my little prof. Your words keep purring so nicely to my ears!

JOHNSON: My Cleo (*hugging her tenderly)* for you no words are sweet enough. I wish I could invent sweeter ones producing sounds as pure as the tinkling of crystals!

CLEO: Oh my Theo, your words are sweet to my ears. You know so much, so much!

JOHNSON: What I knew is very little compared to what I have to learn from your pretty body.

CLEO: Oh my Theo, but it's a body like so many others!

JOHNSON: No, my Cleo, yours is the most precious treasure I could possess. Every innermost recess of it, every inch of your skin is a mystery to me. The more I explore the more I want to explore!

CLEO: Oh my Theo, I love you, and my body is yours! Take it at will!

JOHNSON: (*Aroused*) Oh yes, let's go back to your room. In peace, let me caress your golden body (*they go back into room No. 11 while Da Silva comes out of number 8*).

SCENE VIII

DA SILVA: (*Followed by Gloria*) You see, Lori, I was right. For him days and seasons are of no account any more. Fine! One must take the rough with the smooth, so let's accept him for now. A bet is a bet, is it not? But our friend must quickly go back to his beloved Maiduguri. Otherwise he will strike root here, and roots in the plural you can believe me!

GLORIA: Take roots in the plural for he disturbs me like hell!

DA SILVA: Entertain no fears, dearest Gloria. You will soon be rid of him. The fake convalescence that the doctor gave him will soon expire.

GLORIA: The earlier the better. Let peace reign in our place!

DA SILVA: A bet is a bet, Lori. I had to go right to the end of the experiment, with 50,000 naira at stake! All my friends are going to laugh their heads off when they read the circumstantial report of the actions and doings of this gentleman, from the day of his arrival to his departure. On the other hand the unfortunate punter will have nothing to laugh about!

GLORIA: It would be a monumental joke, mounted by expert hands (*roaring with laughter*) and this so-called professor is more of an ass than of a professor, believe me!

DA SILVA: (*Roaring with laughter*) He believes, really believes that I was a thug and even a pimp, having eleven mistresses. Just imagine eleven mistresses! (*laughing even louder*) When in fact you, my darling is enough to content me. The worst of all is that he believes I'm going to share my entire "harem" with him.

GLORIA: Naivety sometimes knows no limits!

DA SILVA: You couldn't have put it better, dear Lori. He doesn't' realise that the ten girls with you are there not for love but for pure self interest.

GLORIA: The Ninas, the Maggies, are no more than girls without virtue or reputation.

DA SILVA: Come little professor... Come out of your kennel. Come indecent fornicator. Let me put you, manumilitari, on a train for Maiduguri.

(*The curtain falls*)

SCENE IX

(*The platform of Creek town railway station. Johnson is alone in the midst of several suitcases, travelling bags and packages, with a cage containing a parrot*).

JOHNSON: (*Looking at the far end of the stage*) In two days we shall be in Maiduguri, Cleo and I (*pensive*). But what is she doing, my sweet Cleo. All her suitcases are here (*counting them*) one, two, three, four, five, six... That's correct. Even her parrot is here but she herself... Ah she won't be long (*beginning to walk*). In half an hour the train is going to enter the station and take off in ten minutes, if punctual. NRC sometimes has elastic timetables, it's well-known. All the same... Oh how impatient I am to leave with her for Maiduguri, the first stage of a long journey for the two of us, loving forever. Ah, she's still not here! Ah women! Charming creatures but so unpredictable. She's certainly gone to say bye-bye to her friends. Maybe they will come to see her off. Oh my darling Cleo, I have a lump in my throat when I think of you who opened such sweet roads for me! Oh lechery! Oh lovely debauchery! Oh fornication, so sweet that I shall henceforth enjoy at will. Oh mental aberration, beneficial drugs, all of them, and all these, thanks to you Cleo my callpygean Venus who revealed lust, debauchery and the seventh heaven to me! She agreed, the sweet and beautiful Cleo, to come with me to Maiduguri, unite her life with mine. Could there be a better proof of love? To go and bury herself with me in a hole which is no more than sand and dust burning hot like an oven!

SCENE X

JOHNSON:	(*Seeing a group of people coming nearer*) It's her, for sure. I recognise the voices of Amadeus and Cleo (*looking attentively*). Yes, she's the one. In the middle of the group, so beautiful and so lively (*in a loud voice*). Cleo, Cleo!
CLEO:	(*Replying like the echo*) Theo! Theo!
JOHNSON:	Cleo! Cleo!
CLEO:	(*Beginning to run*) Theo, my Theo, I am here all for you (*kissing and hugging him*).
JOHNSON:	And I too am all for you, my sweet Cleo.
CLEO:	We have so much to learn from each other.
JOHNSON:	From you I have learnt how good are those things that people call bad.
CLEO:	And from you I have learnt how sweet and musical is philosophy, and not harsh or grating as dull fools suppose (*train's hooting is heard from afar*)
DA SILVA:	(*Aside*) And I will receive my 50,000 naira, Cleo's departure for Maiduguri being an unrefutable proof. The little prof. has been overpowered by lust. He's going with

Cleo to Maiduguri. Gloria and I are going too, each of us having his or her own reason.
We, to collect our money
Theo for lust galore
As for Cleo it's to learn philosophy
And have another life.
(*The hooting of the approaching train is heard*).

CLEO, GLORIA, JOHNSON, DA SILVA: (*All in a chorus*) For Maiduguri, hi hip hurrah! For Maiduguri, hi hip hurrah!

JOHNSON: Mine is lechery. Hip hip hurrah!

CLEO: Mine is philosophy. Hip hip hurrah!

DA SILVA: Mine is the 50,000 naira. Hip hip hurrah!

GLORIA: The 50,000 naira from this very unusual bet. Hip hip hurrah!

(*The curtain falls*)

ACT II

SCENE I

(*In the sitting room of Zacharia the rich man who originated the bet*).

DA SILVA: (*Followed by Johnson, Gloria and Cleo*) (*to Gloria*) At last in Maiduguri and in Zacharia's palace! You and I have come to collect the amount I won. Fifty thousand naira, that's what it is, quite an amount for me, a drop in the sea for a chap like Zacharia! But such tycoons are very often the stingiest creatures on earth! I am certainly not going to cry! He was sure of himself when the whole affair started!

GLORIA: Well Amadeus, this type of man knows only one thing well, business! His knowledge of human nature is almost non-existent.

JOHNSON: (*To Cleo*) I don't know why Amadeus has asked me to come here. I know that Zacharia all right but we are not on friendly terms, oh no! On the contrary, I hate such people who worship gold, as much as they hate people like me, cultured, learned, wise but poor!

CLEO: We'll soon know! Sure we will.

DA SILVA: (*To Johnson*) My dear Theophilus, I must tell you something now, but before I start you must promise not to hit me, shout at me, or even raise your voice!

JOHNSON: How can I promise without knowing!

DA SILVA: It's an indispensable condition before I can tell.

JOHNSON: Is it so bad? Must there be such a condition to your telling it?

DA SILVA: Bad? Not to me, only to you maybe. Everybody sees things under a different angle!

JOHNSON: Go on then! (*speaking off*) How could I hit him? He is twice as big as me! (*to Da Silva*) Go on! I'll keep quiet! Has it anything to do with our being here?

DA SILVA: It has.... (*embarrassed*) it has even a lot! Well I had better plunge and tell you the whole story!

JOHNSON: Ok! Say what you have to say! You are not usually a shy person!

DA SILVA: (*Laughing*) No, but I feel sort of ashamed to have put you... Eh... involved you in a bet in which you are the moot character!

JOHNSON: Involved me in a bet... without my knowledge or consent!

DA SILVA: I am afraid that is so.

JOHNSON: (*In an angry tone*) Scoundrel! You should indeed be ashamed!

CLEO: Please Theophilus, keep down your temper!

DA SILVA: And keep your promise! Keep quiet!

JOHNSON: How can I keep quiet? Now that I know what you've been up to!

DA SILVA: A promise is a promise! Do you deny that?

JOHNSON: It may be but my hands are itching to slap you, and my feet to kick you!

CLEO: Theophilus! Please!

DA SILVA: Well go on if you so please!

GLORIA: Amadeus please!

JOHNSON: (*Speaking off*) I wish I could knock down the bastard! But how can I knock down a

	mountain of bones and muscles? (*to Da Silva*) Go on! A promise is a promise, I concede.
DA SILVA:	Well! Months ago, Zacharia announced in a party where you were present that no woman could ever lead you astray! I told him that any time anywhere I could make sure that you could succumb to the blandishments of lechery! Zacharia then proposed a bet of ₦50,000 and I accepted it! Send him to me in Creek town and I'll change the identity of the man, I had said pretending I could shape a man like clay figurine! And you came to Creek town and I changed your identity, and you are here with Cleo! A totally new person!
JOHNSON:	And all this without my knowledge! You have no right to make a guinea-pig of me. (*As though infuriated*) I should punish you both one way or another, kick your behind for all you are worth, and send you rolling down a hill of fire. But...
DA SILVA:	But! Go on!
JOHNSON:	But when I put all your devilry on a pan of the weighing scale (*looking at Cleo with adoration*) and the love and affection Cleo gives me on the other, I realize I am on the winning side! And all my fury bid goodbye! (*Laughs*).

DA SILVA: Well, then that bet has enriched both of us!

JOHNSON: Enriched us both?

DA SILVA: You have found love, passion, affection. And I've found kindness from mammon, if indeed it does materialise.

JOHNSON: I've found Cleo no doubt. And Cleo is all I need! But are you going to pocket the entire sum of ₦50,000!

DA SILVA: Indeed. But I also have the satisfaction of being the author of your mutual happiness in love, yours and Cleo's.

JOHNSON: To think that all this was a put up job, a comedy, a farce! I deserve a compensation to say the least!

DA SILVA: A compensation?

JOHNSON: Yes, a compensation! In hard cash! I may have not just changed in my attitude to sex. My change of identity is limitless! It's time I joined the club of business tycoons and crafty crooks. So a commission on that bet of yours is a must for me.

DA SILVA: A commission? In hard cash!

JOHNSON: ,In hard cash! I don't want any dude cheque! And I want 10% commission, no less. I'll not settle for anything less.

DA SILVA: (*As if thinking things over*) One minute! Let me think! I need to ponder a little.

JOHNSON: Please do! Take your time. But be sure I'll settle for nothing less.

DA SILVA: Well Professor, you still have a lot to learn... and I can teach you something. And I would like to, for I feel compassion for you.

JOHNSON: It's 10% I want! Teach me what you will.

DA SILVA: (*Laughing*) Prof! I laugh at you! O let me laugh!

JOHNSON: Laugh all your heart. Laugh on. But know I'll bargain for nothing less.

DA SILVA: You insist on 10% Prof!

JOHNSON: I do! I do!

DA SILVA: (*Laughing still*) Prof! I'll give you 20%, no less.

JOHNSON: 20%! 20%? No less!

DA SILVA: Yes 20%! Which makes ₦10,000! No less!

JOHNSON: ₦10,000! (*apart*) I earn that in six months! (To Da Silva) Why are you so generous!

DA SILVA: I am no crook Theophilus... I am a friend above all. To start with I want you to know that in business if you want 10 ask for 20!

JOHNSON: Thank you! Thank you for your counsel! I'm entering a completely new world! In that new world I acknowledge you as my professor.

DA SILVA: Never too late Prof! I'll hand-over your ₦10,000 to you as soon as I've secured the bet money from Zacharia (*noise outside*). Here he comes... the only loser in that affair!

JOHNSON: He had better pay up without ado! If he does not, we'll be two against one!

(*The Curtain falls*)

SCENE II

ZACHARIA: (*Comes in*) Hello Amadeus! Hello Prof! Happy to see you both.

DA SILVA: Good day Mr Zacharia...

JOHNSON: Good day sir!

ZACHARIA: What can I do for you? To what do I owe the pleasure of your visit?

DA SILVA: It is the bet that has brought us here. The bet you've lost and I've won.

ZACHARIA: The bet! What bet? I never lose any bet. I've never lost any bet.

DA SILVA: Have you forgotten? The ₦50,000 bet on Prof. Theophilus Johnson's lack of interest in women! By making good that lack I was to win the bet.

ZACHARIA: Oh the bet at that party!

DA SILVA: Yes! At that party! Thanks for recalling!

ZACHARIA: Sorry I am so busy right now, jumping from one business conference to another! Was it ₦50,000? Yes it was.

DA SILVA: Well, I've won. You can confirm it from Johnson himself.

ZACHARIA: (*Eying Cleo*) ₦50,000 only! I must have been out of my mind that night! Such a bet is worth far more, I assure you. And I'm not joking.

JOHNSON: Is that so? You mean it? In my new. world, a surprise awaits me at every turn.

ZACHARIA: (*Gloating at Cleo*) Such a bet is worth 6,000 murtalas! 5,000 for you, Da Silva and 1,000 for the worthy Professor!

DA SILVA and JOHNSON: (*Together*) Thank you sir! (*bowing*) Thank you for your good memory! Thank you for your generosity. You're truly magnanimous. You're a true businessman.

ZACHARIA: Who is the lady by the way who has conquered the Prof's heart? She deserves a prize too.

DA SILVA: (*Showing Cleo*) Here she is, Cleo. Dazzling and beautiful as a diamond! She's won his love and he's won hers.

ZACHARIA: *(Mesmerised)* Dazzling and beautiful! (*Speaking off*) And worth becoming one of my numerous girlfriends! Well (*pulling a cheque book from his pocket*), let me settle it... 100,000 naira for you Da Silva, 20,000 for you Prof. and (*making eyes at Cleo and expressive gestures showing his profound interest in her person*) 10,000 for the young lady (*writing a cheque*). Here is yours Da Silva (*writing a second one*), here's yours Prof (*writing a third one*), and yours Cleo... (*handing the cheque to her with his business card attached to it*). Hoping to see you soon! (*Making eyes, in a low voice to Cleo*) Alone! You and me! Without that pauper of a Professor! That dunce!

CLEO: (*Giving back the cheque to Zacharia*) Keep your cheque Mr Zacharia! I'm no part of the deal, a stranger to that bet and not for sale!

ZACHARIA: Sorry young lady. I did not mean to hurt you... all I did and said was in homage to your beauty... Keep the cheque! I beg!

CLEO: Ok I'll keep it as a souvenir... Theo! I'll pin it up on one of our bedroom wall to remind us of the bet... which originated our love and happiness...

JOHNSON: (*Speaking off*) 20,000 naira! A year's salary of a university Prof... when that tycoon can afford to throw away 130,000 naira for a bet! But Cleo was right to refuse his 10,000 naira... should I keep the cheque or like her offer it back to the fellow? (*shaking the cheque*) A year's salary in my hand! A year sweat and headache... (*dashing towards Zacharia*). A year salary gone you hear! (*to Cleo*) Shan't I offer to do what you did? Shan't I offer to return this cheque? I must, I must. Ours is true love. We are not saleable commodities.

CLEO: Yes, yes, do return it to him. He already thinks I'm his mistress and he can do what he likes with me. From his low tones to me and hints of lewdness, it is clear enough... I am not for sale. Nor are you. Ours is true love. Money is secondary. It comes and goes. Let him take back his cheque.

JOHNSON: (*To Zacharia*) Sir, take back your cheque. You didn't lose your bet to me. Give it to your friend Da Silva if you like.

ZACHARIA: (*To Cleo*) (*in low tones*) It's for your sake that I raised the bet amount here and now. Don't throw me overboard. All I have is yours. What do you find in this blake that I haven't? I shall be wholly yours once you're mine.

CLEO: (*Aloud*) Theo, my love, let's get along, for I've seen the face of lechery, and I cannot bear it. Give away the cheque and come.

ZACHARIA: (*Accepting the cheque*) Has money less to offer than sex? If you were wise, Theo, you wouldn't be doing this.

DA SILVA: Sex is one thing, love another. Theo has found love all the way along, for he has known that love is life. Life without love is not worth living. As for money, it is only a means, to be used for life and not the loss of life. You and I are money's slaves. Not Theo. Don't you agree. Gloria.

GLORIA: I do, I do.

ZACHARIA: If he can be corrupted for the sake of sex, he can be corrupted for the sake of money too.

DA SILVA: You can see from their mutual devotion that it is love not sex that has claimed them. So money cannot corrupt those of the long chalk. Want to bet on it (*Theo and Cleo move away, holding hands*).

(*The curtain falls*)

THE LOAFER

CAST

EDWARD: The loafer

REBECCA: His wife

ACT I

SCENE I

The outside of a hut. A coconut tree. A bed. Edward arrives humming a song and holding a bottle of local gin. He lies down on the bed with splayed toes and still holds the bottle. He covers his face with a big straw hat. From time to time he chases away troublesome fly, then he sleeps off, snoring loudly.

His wife arrives and surveys the scene.

REBECCA: The loafer! That's all he knows how to do, lying down, sleeping and praying to God or the devil that no work should come his way. I often wonder how I come to be married to such a chap! He is not a bad sort my Edward, not all! No, of course not. But he can't be bothered with working. Incredible! One would think that he has been bitten by the fly that transmits the sleeping sickness. The tsetse fly, it is called, you know. Furthermore...

EDWARD: (*Dreaming*) Oh! How nice not to do anything while things bustle all around me, and when Rebecca my sweet-natured companion is treating herself to all the work on the farm, and in the house!

REBECCA: (*Facing the audience*) Did you hear that? Oh, the unsavoury individual! The truth comes out, no doubt from the mouth of a dreamer. All the more so when the dreamer has a nearly empty bottle of *ogogoro**in his hand! In Vino Veritas, as they say. In this case, the truth is in *ogogoro!*

EDWARD: (*Still dreaming*) And now my prayer to the Lord! God! My God, above all, do not bring any work today! Keep it till tomorrow, bring instead a bottle full of *ogogoro!*

REBECCA: Can you hear that! Well, well, well! I can recognise him. A loafer! That is what he is! Indeed, indeed, indeed!

EDWARD: (*Still dreaming*) My Lord, let there 'be a strong wind tomorrow, to let fall all the ripe coconuts, so that I do not have to use a long pole to bring them down.

REBECCA: (*Laughs*) Oh! How funny! How funny indeed!

EDWARD: (*Continues his prayer*) My God, let the week have at least six Sundays! And please double the number of holidays!

REBECCA: Oh! The nasty fellow! The pig! Really, he goes too far! To think that at 11.00 a.m. he

---

*Ogogoro: local gin.

is still in bed, sleeping like a dormouse, dreaming aloud, even though I have been up since sunrise! (*shouting in Edward's direction*) You loafer! Your bone-idleness is immeasurably indecent!

EDWARD: (*Responds with a resounding snore*) Rrr... Rrr..

REBECCA: Upon my word! He scoffs at me! Is he perhaps putting on an act, pretending to be sleeping in order to make fun of me?

EDWARD: (*Still dreaming*) I bless Sundays but hold Mondays in contempt! Monday, a real black day! You couldn't call it anything but black! Darker than Rebecca's skin!

REBECCA: Do listen to that! Darker than Rebecca's skin! My God! I have strong desire to give this bastard a good thrashing and send him to the farm to work a little. But since he doesn't know how to do anything with his hands, he will do more harm than good to the poor soil!

EDWARD: (*Still dreaming*) I cannot understand why some people stir so much!

REBECCA: Oh! The beast, the cannibal, I am going to strangle him!

EDWARD: (*After some more snoring*) Rebecca, for example, who is always fidgeting, she gets up at 6.00 a.m. and goes to bed at midnight!

REBECCA: Oh! The swine, the scoundrel! Saying things like that, even though I go through a hell of trouble to feed him and the six children he has saddled me with!

EDWARD: (*Snores*) Rrr.... Rrr..

REBECCA: (*Wanting to wake him up, walks towards him*) Edward! You loafer! (*yelling*) Edward, off with you! Get up!

EDWARD: (*Still in his dream*) Oh! What a beautiful mermaid's voice! Mermaid, this adorable creature that haunts our rivers! We call it *mammy-water* in my village, the daughter of the rivers. She is not like "old mother Hit Hard", this shabby looking old hag that I would drown if I could.

REBECCA: I, Rebecca, "old mother Hit Hard!" I, Rebecca, an old hag! And a very shabby looking one on top of it! And this rotten lot would throw me into the water if he could! Ah! I am prompted to give him such a good hiding that for once I will merit the nickname he has given me. (*Seizing a stick*) And now, let us fight it out, my worthless husband! (*giving him a blow with the stick*) Here, take that this blow, for naming me "old mother Hit Hard!" (*Giving him another blow*) And that one for calling me a shabby old hag!

EDWARD: (*Wakes up with a start*) Ouch! Ouch! Ouch! Oh my ribs, my limbs, my behind, my buttocks! (*giving Rebecca a nasty look*) Old girl are you not crazy to hit your husband so?

REBECCA: My husband? You must be joking! A dormouse, a sleepy head, certainly! (*giving him a final blow*) A suning lizard, for sure, but certainly not my husband!

EDWARD: Ouch!... Ouch! Ouch! Your companion of so many years!

REBECCA: Companion, companion, what a joke! A companion gulping down *ogogoro* like water and tipsy most of the time, when not sound asleep!

EDWARD: The father of your kids!

REBECCA: The father of my kids, true, but it has not given you much work to become all that, eh! Tell me! It has given you pleasure and excitement, that's all, eh! You old bastard!

EDWARD: What's more, shaking the lovely dreams which were running round in my head!

REBECCA: What were you dreaming of? Who were you dreaming about?

EDWARD: Certainly not of you!

REBECCA: Who then?

EDWARD: Does it matter to you? (*taking a bottle of ogogoro and taking a gulp of it*) There's never any enjoyment with you around, one finds oneself in mourning!

REBECCA: How can I, Rebecca, be enjoying myself when I have six brats pulling at my skirts and always demanding to be fed?

EDWARD: (*Taking another gulp of ogogoro*) There, you are exaggerating. But can't you respect the sleep and the dreams of others? Are you jealous of not being able to reach such heights?

REBECCA: How can I attain these so-called heights when I work like a beast of burden from morning till evening? And slaving away for whom? Yes, for whom? For Mr Edward, so as to take care of his needs and those of his kids? Let's not speak of my needs which in any case are minimal, and of which you could not care less! You don't care a dime about my needs! You're interested only in having a good sleep at night, and of course a nice siesta in the afternoon, not forgetting sucking at your bottle of gut rot, your most trusted companion!

EDWARD: What do you expect! At least, it gives me satisfaction without being a pain in the neck as you are.

REBECCA: Me, a pain in the neck, me who is only trying to remind you of your responsibilities as a father and as a husband!

EDWARD: (*Gets up slowly*) Rebecca, what can I do about it? I am born like that, with splayed out toes and a long lasting and incurable laziness! I am a victim, Rebecca. The poor victim of a fate forever vested on me! I was already like that at school. I was never able to learn anything, despite the efforts of the teacher. The poor fellow, tired of reprimanding me without any result, sent me to the far end of the class, under a big ceiling fan. There, I dreamt and slept in absolute tranquillity quite happy at having been kept out of multiplication tables and conjugation of sentences.

REBECCA: Oh! I know all that. I was well warned before our marriage. "Do you love this boy?" I was asked. "Well he will make life difficult for you, as he will never do a damn thing, has never done one all his life, be it at school, during his short stay in the army or elsewhere."

EDWARD: (*Laughs*) That's very true. At school, I didn't do a damn thing. On the other hand, I was an expert at launching all sorts of missiles that I called K.F.O.'s.

REBECCA: K.F.O.'s

EDWARD: Yes! K.F.O.'s, Known Flying Objects! Of course my launching base was at the far end of the class, under the fan...

REBECCA: (*Starts laughing too*) What an odd one you were and still are. And didn't you ever have a dunce's cap?

EDWARD: A dunce's cap, me? I had one on permanently and I was proud of it believe me. Besides that, I didn't allow any competition, believe me. I monopolised the dear dunce's cap from the beginning of the school year to the end. By the way, I still have got it with me (*bringing it out from under his mattress and putting it on*). As you can see! I don't need telling you that I did not care whether Rome was the capital of Italy or of Niger and if 7 times 9 is 63 or 64. "Oh you know," I was telling the school master. "Geography and I are no pals. As for Arithmetic, I must say that we are sworn enemies. Reciting in a drone 2 times 2, 4, 2 times 3, 6 is truly boring and bothering!" I kept telling the guys, "Me! I have my fingers for counting and as long as I can count my old man's sheep, that's enough for me!"

REBECCA: (*Roaring with laughter*) Ah! I can imagine the scene, poor teacher! Faced with dunce like you!

EDWARD: (*Imitating the teacher's voice*) "So you refuse to answer me!" The teacher was saying and me I retorted curtly: "Me, refuse to answer you? But of course not, it is just that I cannot answer your question, sir. Figures cannot keep still in my head. They jump, twirl and dance without clinging anywhere." – "So I'll have to give you zero, and fail you as usual", he had added. - "Fail me old chap," I replied "fail me with one zero, fail me with two, fail me with ten, I don't care. Your zeros," I continued, "cling even less than all your sciences! All your waffles enter by one ear and go out by the other!"

REBECCA: (*Still laughing*) Poor man of science, poor teacher! Poor dunce!

EDWARD: And me, all I was thinking was, "oh! This guy irritates me. He is always putting me in a temper when I require only one thing of him, that he leaves me in peace." But I couldn't be telling him all that, not wanting to hurt him.

REBECCA: That was very nice of you!

EDWARD: What do you expect? I am very understanding, you know, believe it or not. But the poor guy wouldn't let go, he continued his sweet talk. - "Are you not ashamed of yourself?" he blared out. "This is the fifth time that you are repeating the same class!" And I retorted "Ashamed? I am repeating a class, agreed, but do not feel bad about it! You may know that effort and I are not friends! Besides, I have always been like that since my most tender age, so it's certainly not now that I will change." So, beaten, vanquished, the dear old man shouted: "All right! Sit down and wallow in your corner." And I thanked him sarcastically: "Thank you Prof," I was telling him "thanks a lot, let me wallow at ease in my corner for the six months that I still have to stay in your highly esteemed establishment!" And, I was saying to myself, let's hope he leaves me at the far end of the classroom, near my launching pad! (*bringing out a hollow ruler from beneath the mattress*) This is the best peashooter ever to be introduced in a school, and once I loaded it with a paper torpedo, and blew it out, it went bang! Hitting the bull's eye! Just wait and see Rebecca (*he puts the paper cone in the hollow ruler, puffs out his cheeks and blows it out with all his might after having moved away from Rebecca, aiming at her*). Look!

REBECCA: (*Following with her eyes, the trajectory of the paper cone which almost hit her*). Bravo, you haven't lost your touch! What a genius is my dunce! The king of dunces!

EDWARD: You see, I almost hit you!

REBECCA: Indeed! You don't really lack the energy. That much I should know when it comes to making love or playing tricks on somebody! My tricky dunce!

EDWARD: And so! It doesn't hurt anybody, does it? Are you complaining?

REBECCA: I don't complain of your love making, how can I? But of the consequences! Fancy! Six brats standing over me with a man to boot my belly half the time! That's my lot, poor me!

EDWARD: Rebecca, let me tell you how I was kicked out of school! Indeed, I had that honour!

REBECCA: And you are boasting about it! My dear husband is proud of such shameful deeds! Poor dunce!

EDWARD: And so? Can't I be allowed to highlight the little I have done?

REBECCA: Go on! Tell, recite, declaim if it amuses you! Poor dunce knows his own merit, and must no doubt proclaim it.

EDWARD: It's simple, it's short, Rebecca, you'll see. It happened the day one smart guy told on me at school, the dirty sneak! "You'll soon see you bloody jerk!" I started to yell "how I treat the telltales of your kind." I jumped on him. The guy screamed his head off for fear. So loud were his screams that the headmaster who was passing by, heard and saw the whole scene and hurried towards us (*imitating the headmaster's voice*). "Are you not ashamed?" he shouted at me, "for hitting a boy shorter than you by a head!" "Ashamed, me? Not at all!" I replied. "He is going to get a good hiding, the dirty sneak!" "Stop it, I say," he continued "or you will be dismissed immediately!" "Oh great, then!" I replied straight off. "My old man will be very happy. He always complains that school is compulsory! I can even, free of charge, bash in your little head, to be sure of being kicked out quicker." And I was talking as if I had been on familiar terms with the headmaster. Can you imagine that? He couldn't believe his ears! Then I stood up like this, (*making the gesture*) like a boxer, shouting at him! "Come on mate, I leave to you the choice of arms, fists or the whole body, take your pick!" I couldn't care less as I was taller than him by a head. The poor chap was a very small shrivelled man and I am no fool, be it with my fists, my feet or my head.

REBECCA: And you were not ashamed to take advantage of your strength and large size?

EDWARD: Me? Not at all! Small or tall chaps, males or females, it's all the same, I hit! But old girl, it's enough! Let me tell you my story otherwise I'll have to hit you too to make you shut up!

REBECCA: All right if that's how you want it I'll keep quite!

EDWARD: "Neither boxing, nor wrestling," he cried, terrorised. "You know I have no sturdy constitution." "What are you trying to say about your constitution?" I asked him. "Listen to me very well my dear headmaster, it's either one or the other. You throw me out straight away or I bash in your coconut head!" I told him "Well young man", he said, "I cannot but congratulate you, you have at least shown great singleness of purpose and you are not to be easily put off! All right, agreed, I throw you out immediately, you hear me, at once! By the way, young man, you are *de facto* out, legs, fists, head, and all! You see I have complied with your desires! So let's remain good friends!" "Without any nasty blows?" I asked him, "Without the least clout on your ugly mug?" "Without any bashes at all!" he replied. "Of what use will that be since you are already out?" "Then," I said, "I can clear off!" "But of course," he replied straight off. "You can split it, clear off, beat it right now, if you feel like it!"

REBECCA: You must have been very happy!

EDWARD: Happy? That word cannot describe what I felt!

REBECCA: I can well imagine the scene!

EDWARD: I felt on top of the world... and I danced, sang and cried out my joy! Oh great! I was finally free not to do anything, freed of multiplication, and all sorts of tables, addition, substraction, division, multi-headaches that I could not take any more! Bye bye schooling, bye bye teachers! I kept shouting. "What a joy, I am born again!" I went on, you should have seen how that phrase was dancing in my head! But I was disappointed. Oh yes, things had gone too easily and the headmaster had escaped the working over I had reserved for him. Well my dear Rebecca, you have seen how at fourteen I returned to my sheep. They at least respect my sleep, unlike you.

REBECCA: You are starting again? What do you want, my death or what?

EDWARD: Why do you say that? I have to put things straight. O.k! They were nice and gentle, my sheep, I swear!

REBECCA: They had no trouble being gentle, since one say, meek as a lamb! But you have not answered my question. Do you want my death or what?

EDWARD: How could I want your death? Who then would take care of the kids? I'd be forced to work! Can you imagine that? Can you see me slaving away, me, a good for nothing who has never done a damn thing with my ten fingers, either at school or in the army!

REBECCA: The army?

EDWARD: Yes the army! As to the army I really have to tell you about it! You will split your sides laughing. As you know I spent six months of my life with a uniform on my back. I thought I had found a cosy job that will allow me to idle around and get away with it, so I enlisted. But it wasn't at all like that! They wanted me to work my guts out, the rotten bastards! So I did all I could for them to throw me out quickly! Six months after, I had already given back to them uniform, broom, rifle and all the bloody rest even though I had enlisted for a period of two years! Most of the time, I was armed with either a broom or a rifle. The broom scene always took place at the courtyard of the barracks which I was supposed to sweep every morning. But you know me, overtaken by my congenital idling away, I slept standing, and hanging on my broom. (*Taking a broom and miming the scene*) Look! Just like that, chasing away from time to time a troublesome fly which dared to venture on an exposed part of my skin without any respect, just like you by the way, for the sleep of the others. But straight away I was off again to hit the hay, dreaming of civilian life and of bleating ewes!

REBECCA: I wish I could have seen you with your gun or your broom, it must have been quite a sight!

EDWARD: And when the Warrant Officer who was on duty passed and saw me sleeping, clung to my broom, he got annoyed and soon was in a flaming temper, and really cross, and he was yelling like a deaf man. "What! This bastard is still snoozing, damn it!" (*he brings out a whistle from his pocket*) And the rowdy fellow brought out a whistle from his pocket, still screaming that one would see whether the guy I was, would or not resist the charming voice of his whistle. (*He puts the whistle to his mouth and blows several times with all his strength*) And naturally I woke up with a start. What is it? Who? Where? What? What's that again? Damn it! I hollered out. When I saw the Warrant Officer in front of me, red with anger and bent under the weight of his medals, I put on an act and stammered excuses, "Sor... sorry, sorry, sorry sir. I was dreaming of my country, of my poor mother, oga sir and of my poor father, who are so unhappy to be separated from me and who are waiting for me to help them on the farm."

REBECCA: You! Helping them on the farm? You! (*Bursting out laughing*) Let me laugh!

EDWARD: Well believe you me, that's exactly what the Warrant Officer was thinking! "You help them!" the bastard bellowed, "you who I often catch sleeping hitched onto your broom!" "Oh, oga sir," I replied, using my most tearful voice, "I sleep so little hitched onto my broom" The silly old potbellied fellow replied," "So little? You dare say, so little? You whose snoring could be heard a hundred paces away! This time I will have to report you! Sleeping on duty! That's a criminal offence. It should fetch you a month or two in prison." I did everything to make him relent, buttering him up, dropping soft words in his ears, "my Warrant Officer sir, my Warrant Officer sir. Sir, be understanding and compassionate," I said to him. I am cursed with this terrible laziness right from birth! And it has followed me ruthlessly, making of me a slave who prefers to have his eyes shut rather than open and the body lying rather than upright."

REBECCA: For once you were telling your superior the absolute truth!

EDWARD: But he did not believe me, the bastard! "You are making fun of me," the chap replied aggressively. "Your body lying horizontally, when you are supposed to be active and upright, a broom or a rifle in your hand!" I answered with a plaintive tone, "But sir! But sir!" He continued "you won't be sent down for two or three months but for six, my dear chap, for failing to respect a superior!" I then told myself that I had to switch to a proper level in buttering him up and slipping soft words in his ears. So I took my most humble appearance, addressing him as my lieutenant." "My lieutenant," I told him with a tremor in my voice, "me, to make fun of you, me? Not at all, not the least in the world, my lieutenant!" I saw his expression slowly transformed into a smile. The big fat slob must have been flattered to have been called my lieutenant!

REBECCA: So, in the end what was the dunce's sentence?

EDWARD: Me? I got nothing as you will see. He must have told himself, "That changes everything. If he calls me my lieutenant, it means he is capable of appreciating my real value!" In any case? I was ready to go as high as my captain, had it been necessary. So I whispered "My lieutenant, you have to believe me, I have told you the truth, nothing but the truth. I was born like that. My poor mother herself told me that so many times throughout her short life." Then he really started laughing. It's with a jovial air that he said to me, "Well, you can go. I am magnanimous today and in a good mood!" But I knew that deep down inside he was telling himself, "He called me lieutenant, so that changes everything! "His my lieutenant must earn him due leniency." He must have added, "I am willing to overlook your intolerable behaviour this time, but if I catch you again sleeping, hitched to your broom or your rifle, I will send you to the nick where the unruly are dealt with!" I made a pretence of protesting "Me! My lieutenant? Me who is as meek as a lamb, and who has only one longing. To go back to my flock?"

REBECCA: Edward, you know how to flatter people and moreover you do the same with me but instead of my lieutenant, my lieutenant, it's "my little darling," "my pet" that you shower on me!

EDWARD: Him on the other hand had no idea how to flatter somebody, sharp-tongued as he was! "Come on," he said finally, "take your broom!" I grabbed the broom with my two hands as never before and yelled "yes my lieutenant!" He continued, the bastard, "hold it well! Use both your hands". I continued with "yes my lieutenant," yes my lieutenant" as long as the lesson he wanted me to swallow lasted. As a grand finale, he hollered, the fat beast: "At my command!" I also hollered straight off. "Yes my lieutenant!" He went on to scream, as loudly as before, "sweep! one, two, one, two! Sweep! You lazy bones! Sweep you loafer!" And I swept. Oh my God! And I swept at full speed like a mad man, repeating without stopping "yes my lieutenant, yes my lieutenant!" When I think that this swine was feeling on top of the world because I was calling him my lieutenant, thus flattering his outrageous vanity, I feel mad! From that day onwards, they wanted to turn me into a robot, either him, the bogus lieutenant, the corporal or the sergeant! One, two, one, two!" They kept shouting even though I'd had more than I could take of the broom and the rifle. I had got to the stage of loathing all these chaps in uniform who represented a serious threat to my mental equilibrium! Me, I have a passion for guitar, and not for broom or rifle!

REBECCA: My God that's true, you can handle a guitar!

EDWARD: Oh yes... In that field, I excel (*taking his guitar hung up on the bed and strumming a tune*). And as I love singing; the two go together (*singing a song*) I even have a good voice I am told. As for playing cards I am the expert. Give me a pack and you will see how I work wonders! I will spare you the dices, be they fixed or not. I am the champ in that domain! Well Rebecca, in spite of all that I am the misunderstood guy, that's what I am, misunderstood by you and by the army people in particular, who are thick as a stronghold wall and not the least a bit bright!

REBECCA: You, misunderstood by me? Me who always try to come to your level!

EDWARD: Not always Rebecca, you must confess! Well those blokes.... You hear me, it took them four months to realise that they could never instil in me the love of the broom, this devil of a broom, this thrash of a broom, this rotten broom, this sluttish broom (*Throwing it away)* This blasted broom, this bloody broom (*giving it a kick)*, this mark of servitude, reminiscent of slavery. At the end of six months, they kicked me out, accusing me of being a bad example to my mates. Quite happy I gave back to them their rags, broom, rifle and the whole junk, finding myself as free as a bird, behind the bottom of my sheep to daydream, to sleep, dragging on my incurable laziness as the days went by!

REBECCA: (*Apart*) To daydream, sleep, that's what my dear husband enjoys most and to keep going with that incurable laziness which plagues him so much as the days go by! I

	have a strong desire to send him packing from my house, but I don't know how to start! (*aloud*) And what came next!
EDWARD:	Then, honey, came our marriage and our conjugal life. I have proved to you since that I could be as active in the night as lazy in the day and this is to your profit and delight! Am I right?
REBECCA:	To my profit? Profit indeed! Oh! Let's speak of my profit! Some brief embraces, a fleeting pleasure, oh for that yes! But what more?
EDWARD:	Brief? Embraces that lasted the whole night! Fleeting? Orgasms that sent you to the seventh heaven, so many times the same night! Can you forget? Could I forget?
REBECCA:	(*Sardonically*) To the seventh heaven indeed! And with what reward at the end of it all? One, two, three, six bawling brats that are never satisfied, hanging flaccid breasts, and a silhouette that gives you the creeps!
EDWARD:	Six adorable little lads all of them the spitting image of their dad!
REBECCA:	Good heavens no! They may resemble any other person, ok, but certainly not you. Or

	I'll have seven loafers to feed for the rest of my life.
EDWARD:	Stop it, please! I am tired of hearing such rubbish!
REBECCA:	Well, it's not difficult to tire you, you suffer, my dear, from an acute, chronic, congenital fatigue!
EDWARD:	You are tiring me now. Moreover, you are getting on my nerves.
REBECCA:	Getting on your nerves? That's something new. You're hardly of the nervous and spirited kind, far from it! You are more truly indolent and sluggish!
EDWARD:	(*Exploding with anger and beating at his chest*) Indolent me? Me indolent? Sluggish me? (*Jumping out of the bed*) You'll see, old hag, if I'm indolent. I'll get at your hide! Indolent me! (*takes up a stick and gives her substantial blows on her buttocks*) Take some of that in the meantime!
REBECCA:	(*Howling as if flayed alive*) Help! Help! He's killing me.
EDWARD:	(*Administers more blows*) Take that too, old girl. So you can cry for a good reason!

REBECCA: Edward, I beg of you to be sensible! I warn you. You dunce!

EDWARD: Begging yet warning! (*somehow he stops his hand*).

REBECCA: I am no beggar you brute! Be warned I say.

EDWARD: Woman! Know that I am the master here! I can beat you when I want, (*showing her his stick*) and here is my sceptre! (*lying down again*) Master, as the miller in his own mill! Stop your futile cackling and let me snooze when I feel like it or knock off a bottle of *ogogoro* when I am in the mood.

REBECCA: (*Pretending to be subdued*) Do what you want, Edward dear (*speaking off*). Since there's little else he can do! But if the brute beats me again...

EDWARD: (*Apart*) Here at least is another language altogether! (*with a voice that does not admit any protests*) Come on, go about your business and prepare for me a plate of beans, just as I like them! What I have said must be done.

REBECCA: (*Aloud*) All right darling (*speaking off*). Yes I must let the dunce keep to his level!

EDWARD: (*His head resting on his hands, the right leg in the air resting on the knee of his left leg*) Stop pestering me, you hear! And above all, do not wake me under any pretext!

REBECCA: (*Goes out and speaks off*) Even my death could not wake him up!

EDWARD: (*With a big smile on his lips*) I am the king... and from the bed which is my throne, I reign! (*stifling a yawn*) A gulp of *ogogoro* and his majesty will finally be ready to rest (*producing yawns more and more pronounced*). A royal sleep, in a royal peace, that's exactly what I need most... I, the king... (*sleeping off and beginning to snore like an organ pipe, then to dream*) I the king... Rebecca, do you hear me? Do not wake me up and do not bother me under any pretext! What I say (*his snoring intensifies as the curtain falls*) must be done. Done!

THE CHEATS

CAST:

JOHN GODWIN: A shady businessman

PATIENCE: Godwin's wife

TITUS: Dealer in technical goods

FRIDAY: Godwin's Driver

THE NEW COMER: An employee of the "rent a car" firm

ACT I

SCENE I

JOHN: (*On the threshold of his house speaking to Patience his wife*) By God's grace! Whatever business I do, we cannot save a kobo! Where was the good time when I was a practising lawyer, successful, respected, and honoured?

PATIENCE: You have lost the reputation you had of being a shrewd lawyer. There was a time when everybody wanted you as their legal adviser and advocate to win their cases in court, and draft agreement! And the two of us were invited to every posh party in town, not to speak of the official parties where I was the No. 1 lady! Now you are just a "HAS BEEN", a lawyer without any case, obliged to do small businesses to make a living! Oh! My God! I am ashamed to go down to town in that old and battered car of yours which shows so well how poor we are!

JOHN: Patience, please! Don't add to my problems. All you have said is true... But things are difficult. Don't you know our country is plagued with a serious economic crisis? Are you blind? You should be happy to have a Mercedes car, even an old one, at your disposal... If you knew the number of people who had a vehicle before, and who now are obliged to take a taxi!

PATIENCE: Don't talk rubbish, and don't lecture me! You are just a loafer, even worse. What do you have in mind to improve our social position? Look at my two sisters, both unmarried, and both driving sports cars, and living in luxury flats with posh furniture, two housemaids, one cook and God knows what...

JOHN: Oh, let's speak of your sisters, one is always ready to open her thighs if big money is there, the other is involved in a dirty business I don't want to talk about, which might one day bring her to a firing squad!

PATIENCE: You dare call my elder sister a prostitute? And my younger one a drug pusher? I'll tell you what you really are – a cheat and a crook, of small calibre!

JOHN: Of very small calibre, thank you! I like that! I see where you are driving at! You want me to become a crook of big calibre, a gangster in short, and all that to satisfy your appetite for expensive foods and

	drinks and your greed for money! Well count me out!
PATIENCE:	Is that your last word? I want to live, you hear, and live well. I am still a young woman, full of sex appeal, who can remarry at will. Many tycoons will be too happy to have me as their wife.
JOHN:	You make me laugh... my dear! Sex appeal... sex appeal... after two hours every day in front of your mirror, and so many hours every week at the beauty parlour. It must be a gigantic work the poor people have to produce, to help you keep your so-called sex appeal... Look at your bum full of fat, and at your boobs falling like empty socks. My God!
PATIENCE:	Shut up or I'll scratch your eyes! And answer my question! What do you intend to do to improve our social position?
JOHN:	I cannot pull out an idea from my hat just like that! I want to keep you, Patience, I love you, and cannot stop thinking of our two beautiful kids who are at school in Britain!
PATIENCE:	I feel the same John. I love you too, but we are caught up in the system. We are so

	used to luxury that we cannot accept to live as poor people any more.
JOHN:	Patience, give me a month, and you will be proud of my achievements.
PATIENCE:	Agreed John... my big John... one month... not a day more! (*they kiss tenderly and John goes out*).
PATIENCE:	(*Speaking off*) The message has gone home. I know my John. He needed a push. Now let's see what will come out of all this.

(*The curtain falls*)

SCENE II

Curtain rises showing a shop displaying house appliances and sound equipment. Titus, the owner of the shop is sitting behind his desk. John enters, lifts his arms as if for an embrace and calls the shopkeeper by name.

JOHN: Titus! My dear! How are you after so many years? How are your good father, kind mother and the family? By God the more it goes, the more you look alike. You could pose as your father you know, if not for the difference of age. Terrific! It's a long time since we met, I was abroad, you know. Do you remember me at all?

TITUS: (*In doubt*) Vaguely, but I could not put a name on your face.

JOHN: Well, John Godwin is my name. Do you remember now? We were at Secondary School together in Lagos.

TITUS: (*Still in doubt but pretending to know*) Oh yes I remember now. We were young then.

JOHN: But you are still young. Titus! Don't think you are old. It's the quickest way to become an old man in no time. Well, my dear Titus, your shop is superb! Well-stocked! I have come

	to the right place. I'll be so pleased to do business to a good friend of yesteryears.
TITUS:	Yester what?
JOHN:	Oh! Yes-t-er-years or, if you prefer, the past years. You have all the things I need. Refrigerators, deep freezers, air-conditioners, fans, television sets, gas cookers... Well! Well! Well! You are going to do the biggest sale of your life, my good Titus, and cash down! I only pay cash you know! But I like your goods. They are the best make in town. Your shop is beautiful, super. I need all these to furnish the new house I bought just two days ago. What a refrigerator my God! So big! So well finished! I'll take two, not one. One for the kitchen, one for the sitting-room. Deep freezers? Two for the kitchen, I have so many visitors. Bottle coolers? Two, one for the bar outside, one for the sitting room. Air conditioners? Six, one for each of the bedrooms, one for the sitting room and two for the master bedroom. Ceiling fans? One dozen of the best type. Gas-cookers? One big one for the kitchen, a small one for the pantry. Television? Six small ones, one for each bedroom, two big ones, one for master bedroom and one for T.V. room, video set, two of the best make. Well, I think that this will be all for today. If I need

	more things I'll come back. Have you taken good note of my order? Eight items, forty pieces, is it correct?
TITUS:	(*Making a quick calculation*) Eight items correct, but I find only thirty pieces.
JOHN:	Count again. I am sure of my figures I calculated before coming here.
TITUS:	Correct. Forty-one pieces, I was confused by the one dozen ceiling fans.
JOHN:	Well, now let us talk about money? Show me your price list.
TITUS:	Here it is... (*he hands over his price list*).
JOHN:	(*Putting on an act*) But your prices are simply exorbitant! How come? You will have to give me a big discount.
TITUS:	But my dear John, business is difficult these days. We hardly make two ends meet. Well, I'll give you two and half per cent discount because we are good friends of yest... how did you say?
JOHN:	(*Articulating each syllable*) Yes..ter..years. But forget about your two and half per cent. It's twenty-five per cent I want, no less.

TITUS:	Impossible! You want to skin me alive? Twenty-five per cent! My God what shall I give to my dear wife and my six children to eat? Not to lose this business, I'll give you five per cent.
JOHN:	All right! I do not want to waste your time, nor mine, make it twenty per cent!
TITUS:	Seven and half per cent!
JOHN:	Fifteen per cent!
TITUS:	Ten per cent!
JOHN:	Ok it's a deal. I'll accept ten per cent. Prepare your invoice, and give me that small portable radio free of charge, as a gift to a dear friend of yes..ter..years!
TITUS:	Agreed! You purchase a lot and you pay cash! I like cash, more than cheque, and I hate credit (*he starts writing the invoice*). Well it amounts, after the rebate of ten per cent, to ₦81,899.15.
JOHN:	I knew that you would give me that radio for the sake of our long friendship.
TITUS:	(*Looking pleased*) Yes, you are right, for the sake of our long friendship. I am pleased and honoured that you chose my shop to

	buy so many goods: eight items, forty-one pieces.
JOHN:	(*Taking his cheque book from his pocket*) You said ₦81,899.15, is it not? (*he starts to write the cheque*).
TITUS:	But what are you doing? (*furiously*) What does that mean? You told me that you were paying cash?
JOHN:	Well, I am giving you a cash cheque which you can cash immediately if you go to my bank, in this very town. But take it easy! Where is that long friendship of yours? Vanished? Because of a cheque?
TITUS:	But to-day is Saturday and all the banks are closed!
JOHN:	To-day is Saturday? Are you sure? I still think it is Friday. In any case it does not matter. Sure that you are going to trust me for such a small amount? What is ₦81,899.15 for a big businessman like you?
TITUS:	Such a small amount! By God! ₦81,899.15 a small amount?
JOHN:	If you don't trust me, tear your bill and let us forget about the whole matter! I feel

| | confident that anyone else will be too pleased to make such a sale, against a good cheque, well-written and signed by me. Tell me Titus, is it your last word? You a friend of yesteryears? |

TITUS: But the sum is large, may be not for you, but for me! ₦81,899, almost ₦82,000 is a huge amount! To my knowledge such a sum does not fall from the sky, nor grow in any field!

JOHN: Alright! Let us forget about it. You made me lose my precious time, me an honest and honourable person, whose car alone is worth ₦150,000, and whose house is over ₦1,000,000.

TITUS: (*To himself*) ₦150,000 only in a car! ₦1,000,000 for a house, ₦81,000 is little compared to these sums. To lose such a sale, my God! Let us see that car of his (*he goes out and comes back almost immediately*).

(*Aloud*) Alright I accept. I'll take a chance! Write your cheque while I go to the toilet. (*He goes out)* At the same moment, a man enters, looking furious, and walks in the direction of John.

JOHN: (*Putting a finger on his lips and speaking in a low voice to the new comer*) Keep cool

                        brother, if it is for the counterfeit notes I
                        gave you by mistake, I am very sorry. Give
                        them back to me and have genuine ones
                        instead (*he gives him some banknotes which
                        he takes from his right side pocket and takes the
                        counterfeit ones and puts them in his left pocket*).
                        I noticed it only this morning. Very sorry
                        indeed! When I catch the bastard who gave
                        them to me, I'll beat him proper, before
                        handing him over to the police.

THE NEW COMER: (*In low voice*) Alright, the matter is closed.
                        By the way does the Mercedes which you
                        hired yesterday give you entire satisfaction?
                        Do you know that it is the latest model
                        and the best in the market?

JOHN: (*Still in a low voice*) I am quite happy
                        indeed, thank you very much, and now
                        will you excuse me as I am very very busy.
                        Please this way! (*he virtually pushes the
                        employee of the car hire company out of
                        the shop, glancing all the time behind him to
                        see if Titus can see them or not*)(*speaking off*) I
                        had a narrow escape! (*mopping his forehead
                        with a handkerchief*). If Titus had overheard
                        us my plans were all shattered! (*he comes
                        back to the shop and awaits the return of Titus
                        still mopping his face. Titus comes in. He is all
                        smiles, definitely happy at his big sale*).

TITUS: Have you written your cheque?

JOHN: (*Aloud*) Here it is. Well-written and signed. Please present it early in the morning on Monday! I am very sorry brother to have taken Saturday for Friday (*speaking off*). He will have to run very fast and very far to get his money, because this cheque is a dud cheque, it is not even from my own cheque book. I picked it up from the pocket of a gentleman who was so drunk, that he did not notice anything, when I relieved him of his money, papers and incidentally cheque books. Tomorrow I'll be far away with the hired Mercedes, refrigerators, air conditioners and all the rest! Brocades, laces, gold jewels, silver jewels and all the rest! Diamonds, saphires, turquoises, and all the rest! Not forgetting the 1000.00 dollars I bought too with counterfeit money! None of the salesman saw anything, except that chap from the 'rent a car company' (*laughing*). All these gentlemen must be short-sighted and too mean to buy a pair of good glasses! What about the 20,000 pounds sterling and all the rest! The 10 million C.F.A. and all the rest! And what about the brand new lorry, which will prove very useful to carry all these goods far from here, bought too with counterfeit money! I am really a clever chap, am I not? I have cheated them all, proper, I am the king of the cheats! And now let us go and see Patience, my kind wife, who is waiting for me in the house I rented for one month, with good money this time, and the only time by the way, and who must have already received the largest part of the booty (*John aloud to Titus*). Bye bye brother! Have my things loaded immediately in the lorry waiting outside. Friday, my driver, will supervise the loading. You will see my dear Titus the advertisement I'll make for you. Your sales will jump sky-high and double or triple! I am really grateful for your help. Once more a thousand thanks and all the best!

FRIDAY: Sir, I am here... tell me what to do.

JOHN: Load all these goods in the lorry and drive immediately to my house.

FRIDAY: Ok sir (*John goes after having seen labourers loading the lorry*).

SCENE III

At John Godwin's Rented House

JOHN: Well, my darling Patience, are you happy? Rich we are, if we manage to leave that place unnoticed between now, Saturday noon, and Sunday midnight and have a thousand miles between, the pursuers and us, two poor victims of the hazards of bourgeois capitalism! The so-called businessmen, shopkeepers, traffickers, tricksters, looking for their paraphernalia, brocades, diamonds, T.V and all the rest... us trying to be free and make the two ends meet.

PATIENCE: Congratulations, my dear, you have been very active all these days, considering the quantities of the goods stored here.

JOHN: Yes! But it is not finished yet, wait and see. By the way, have you listed all the articles already here? There are many, you know, and more are to come, of the value of over ₦80,000. We are millionaires, my dear, multi-millionaires even... But all is in kind, except the 100,000 American dollars... pounds, C.F.A. and all the rest! It

	means we have to resell the lot, quickly, at the best price possible.
PATIENCE:	Where are we going to store all these in the meantime?
JOHN:	Do not bother! I have arranged everything. All of the booty, Mercedes, diamonds, lorry, T.V., refrigerators, fans, air conditioners, cookers, furniture, and all the rest, will have vanished in a matter of days, next door in a neighbouring country... We'll only keep a few diamonds, for you my dear, some other jewels, a bundle of brocade of the best quality, so that you can be dressed like a queen!... The 100,000 dollars, 20,000 pounds sterling, 10 million C.F.A. will enable us to vanish at will.
PATIENCE:	Where to?
JOHN:	Name it! What do you prefer? America, Jamaica? New York? Kingston? Jazz or Reggae? There we'll take another identity... You and me are natural comedians. We can in a very short time speak with the same accent and act the same way as any English speaking black man on earth!

PATIENCE: It is Jazz John! America! That's my choice. It is New York, John! This is where I would like our new heaven to be!

JOHN: Alright for Jazz when I have sold T.V., video, vehicles, and all the rest, next door. We'll fly to New York not from Lagos oh, no! We may be wanted there, but from Douala or Abidjan.

PATIENCE: From Abidjan, John! I have always been told that you can buy fashionable clothes there, and I want to set foot on American soil as a queen! No less!

JOHN: Don't be silly! Big girl! We'll have to keep a low profile for some time you know, not to attract the attention of police, customs or any of these fools in uniform.

PATIENCE: Let us celebrate this John... I did put a bottle of champagne in the ice bucket to that effect since yesterday (*she goes out and comes back brandishing a bottle of champagne*).

JOHN: (*Taking the bottle from her hands*) Let me open it, baby... You may make a mess out of it and all the precious liquid may flow out, wasted!.. (*he opens it and the cork pops out faintly*) It must be flat or almost flat... Where did you get it from?

PATIENCE:	As usual, from one of these hawkers in the town dealing in smuggled goods.
JOHN:	I hope that it is not of bad omen! My God! My God! A bottle of flat champagne to celebrate our success! Well, in any case, let's drink to my achievements (*they drink... and the curtain falls*).

SCENE IV

At Kirikiri Prison

(The curtain rises again, and behind the bars we can see Patience and John in prisoners' garb busy in a hot argument).

JOHN:	It was really a bad omen, that cork and that flat champagne!
PATIENCE:	You are a good for nothing as always! You have messed up everything. You are always overconfident and now where are we? Instead of being in New York we'll be ten years in Kirikiri for qualified theft, cheating, forgery and all the rest!
JOHN:	And all the rest, and all the rest! You are the one responsible for our misfortune... You greedy bitch! You pushed me to do all these crimes... the judge should have sent you to the gallows! Is it my fault if at the border they suddenly changed all the police and customs officers?
PATIENCE:	Shut up you moron! Nit cretin! I would have sent you to the firing squad had I been the judge! *(they start to fight with fists and claws and we hear cries of pain).*

A WARDER: (*Rushing towards them*) Stop it, you two! It is too late to blame each other, though not too late I hope, to realise that *crime does not pay!*

(*The curtain falls*)

AVARICE

CAST:

MAROWACI: Father of Bukar and Binta

JAMILA: His wife

BUKAR: His daughter

BINTA:

THE BORROWER

1ST BANDIT

2ND BANDIT

VOICES IN THE CROWD OF SPECTATORS

ACT I

SCENE I

Marowaci's Office, sparsely furnished

MAROWACI: (*Shouting to the wings*) That's two weeks, do you realise, two weeks since that pig of a Tahiru owes me ₦200. Of these two weeks, I haven't slept a single minute! Imagine, ₦200, a tidy sum in the hands of the bandit! For ages! Two weeks! Two weeks at 10% monthly interest, my usual lending rate. That's a lot of money! I know for a fact he won't pay me the interest! O God I could easily have lent out my ₦200 as usual! Doing that to me! (*wild gestures*) ₦200... oh! (*piercing cries*) I've not only lost sleep over it but my appetite! Ah, my ₦200... Oh my God!

VOICE IN THE CROWD OF SPECTATORS: ₦200! But that's nothing, my poor fellow! Why shout out so loud? Many a fellow earns that much in a day! Skin flint! Miser! Scrooge! Shylock! Harpagon!

MAROWACI: (*Shouting*) Oh you! (*apart*) Harpagon? Shylock? Scrooge? What does he mean?

Never heard such names before! Do be quiet! Shut up! Maybe you don't know how hard it is to earn a living! (*to the wings*) It's a crime to disturb the quiet life of an honest man like me, who has a tired and delicate heart! (*to himself*) And my ₦200. How insecure is that bandit Tahiru's claws! God! Swine! Bush pig! Who came begging for a loan to be paid back in three days! And to think I was stupid enough to agree to this loan without interest! I've a kind heart, that's my problem! Well that's the reward I get! The three days have already turned into fifteen! A clear-cut loss of (*counting half aloud and waving his hands around*) ₦2, oh ₦5, oh, oh, oh, ₦5!

A CHEEKY VOICE IN THE AUDIENCE: Your kind heart! Oh come off it!

ANOTHER VOICE: ₦5! I earn that in 5 minutes! Why make so much fuss about it? Crackpot! Loony!

MAROWACI: (*Replying*) You! That's enough! (*to himself*) ₦5, oh! Five good naira in notes... five one naira notes or ten fifty kobo notes, gone, evaporated! Oh! (*tapping his chest*) My poor old heart worn out by all the assaults dealt out by the sharks this earth's infested with!

A VOICE: Shark you yourself are, Marowaci! You who lend out money as a usurer and double your capital in less than twelve months!

MAROWACI: (*To the wings, laughing*) In ten, not twelve! You ill-informed nincompoops! (*to himself*) Oh yes! My heart is broken, crushed by small mishaps! Oh, I'd cry about it if only I'd any tears left!

A VOICE: Crocodile tears of course!

MAROWACI: (*Pretending to throw something in the direction of the voice*) Oh, you be quiet! You're starting to get on my nerves! (*to himself*) Where was I? Oh yes, my broken heart, beaten by chronic insomnia!

VOICE: And all this drama for ₦5! Poor chap, loser, pimp!

MAROWACI: Oh damn! What more! Why are they after me like that? Pests! (*noticing a beggar approaching him with his bowl*) Let me vanish before this scruff tries to get some money out of me! (*going in the opposite direction*) Every time I spot one of these comedians, I must make a detour to avoid them! The few coins I might be weak enough to give him are better off in my pocket than his! Oh yes, what would he do with them! Only get drunk, smoke, take drugs or become addicted to some other vice! If he comes upon me unawares, I'll give him the sermon of his life and counsel him to do like me and economise over every penny and work his way up to my position with patience and self-privation!

VOICE: To your position? One can hardly be proud of it! Your life is nothing but a series of villainous shameful deeds!

MAROWACI: (*Looking as if to kill him*) Another! There's a whole band of them scattered in the crowd! And not to sing my praises either! More likely the opposite. They insult me, threaten me, throwing the vilest words, the worst lies and calumnies at my face! Me, a usurer? Me, a miser? Me, with a wife and kids! (*counting his fingers*) I've five of them, four boys and a girl, and who feeds them all! And who feeds the mother? Oh yes! It's I who feed her! I don't discriminate! Were I a miser would I care for such a brood? Were I a miser would I have four boys and a girl? Of course not! The marriage of four girls would have brought me a fortune. Instead the boys are going to cost me a fortune! It's nothing but a pack of lies when they talk of me being a miser! As for usury, I only do what is necessary. I am conserving my capital, assaulted from all sides by every scrounger who steals from me, by bad prayers, and by galloping

	inflation which in time erodes the most stable capital. Lying fools, that's what they all are. It would be alright if they were content to threaten me, but no, they watch my every move, waiting to jump on me to steal, snatch, or rob!
A VOICE:	How can anyone steal from someone who keeps everything under lock and key and is perpetually on the alert?
MAROWACI:	You hear that? Judas! (*in a low voice looking fearfully around*) I'm obliged to keep my money at home! The banks? They're but thieves and co! It's they who practise usury! They receive your money, use it, yet charge you a fee for doing that. The list of the kinds of fee they charge is a mile long. Bank charges, commission on turnover, and I don't know what else without ever giving you a kobo of interest, while they lend out at 25% or even 30%.
A VOICE:	But you lend out at 10%!
MAROWACI:	Listen to them! You'd think they know more about my business than I do! (*quietly*) But how do they know I lend money at 10% a month? Maybe through clients who have complained about my high rates (*thoughtful*) High rates! They've only to take my place for a week! They'll see what

	happens to 10% a month! They melt quicker than snow in the sun, the bite of a bad payer being worse than a sun-burn. Anyway, who cares about all these dogs? Let them bark! As for the clients, that is another race of dogs, prudence, my friends, is the way out. They're more likely to assail you than defend you! (*noticing his wife appearing*) Well, here's the mother of my children! What a pity you can't have kids without a wife! A wife is at the least inexhaustible source of expense!
VOICE:	The fun you have in bed – doesn't that count!
MAROWACI:	Him again (*sighing*). He's stuck to me like a leech! The fool! (*after a silence*) All women aim high, the bitches! Only the most expensive things attract them, and they're very alert when it comes to spending! When it's a matter of earning, saving, producing, they're a lot less dynamic, readily sliding into laziness! She's not yet so close, yet I can sense from her expression that she's going to ask for money! And she certainly doesn't go in for half measures on such occasions! Ten, twenty, thirty naira she will demand without batting an eyelid, without any shame and without fear of being rebuffed! She's got a nerve, the bitch! For me, such a moment is the worst. When

I have to hand out ten, twenty, thirty naira, it's as if a thousand flames were searing my body! (*to his wife who is now close to him*) Wife! There you are! How are you this morning? And what brings you here so early? You aren't ill I hope? Are the children not well? Do they have a fever or a cut?

JAMILA: The dear angels are all fine! In the best of spirits.

MAROWACI: Are they being naughty? Would they abuse their dear mother or their kind and indulgent father?

JAMILA: The little angels are as sweet as they could be! I haven't come to complain about them. Far from it.

MAROWACI: So what's the problem?

JAMILA: It's a question of money, dear husband.

MAROWACI: (*Howling as if strangled*) A question of money! Money you say? Oh, oh, oh! (*to the wings*) What did I tell you?

JAMILA: Money - and not just a little!

MAROWACI: (*Who has misunderstood*) Oh, just a little, that's better. That's better.

JAMILA: No just a little, a lot, do you hear! (*aside*) It's amazing how the ears would hear what they want to hear!

MAROWACI: What? Not a little, a lot! Damnation!

JAMILA: Yes, a lot of money! A lot believe me!

MAROWACI: (*To the wings*) What did I tell you? Women, a breed of she-hyenas, run around with their claws out to strip you, fleece you, skin you alive, in short bankrupt you (*laughter in the audience*).

VOICE: You make us laugh old chap!

MAROWACI: Silence please, and stop laughing, the matter is serious! (*to his wife*) So you said "a lot of money?" Didn't you mean just a little? Haven't you made a mistake by saying 'lot' instead of 'little'?

JAMILA: There's no mistake! I said what I meant, and what's more, the word 'lot' isn't enough to describe my needs.

MAROWACI: (*Frightened*) My very dear wife, how much do you mean? (*to himself*) How much can she mean, if "a lot" isn't enough? I'm going to have to defend myself step by step to cut down the demands of this woman. My! How awful to be constantly assailed like that! (*to his wife*) Well dear I am all ears. What do you want? Be brief, don't waste my time and yours and tell me of your needs in a word!

JAMILA: (*To the wings*) If I were as economical with my words as he is with all his possessions – money, food, linen, clothes – then our conversation would be but a sign language! (*to her husband*) I need ₦200 urgently for...

MAROWACI: (*Interrupting*) ₦200! (*modulating his voice*) 200!, 200, you say? You really said 200? Could you possibly have said 200? (*Walking up and down*) Oh! Oh! Oh, 200? I can't believe my ears! My poor ears are buzzing so much that it hurts? To think that these three words, two hundred naira, said one after another are more noisome than the cathedral bells!

JAMILA: It is really ₦200 I'm asking for, not a penny more, not a penny less! Believe me, if your ears buzz so loud because of 200 miserable naira, they'll certainly burst when I ask for thousands, which will be quite soon, given the galloping inflation raging all about us.

MAROWACI: What are you saying? Inflation! One thousand naira! You want to kill me? (*to *the wings*) She wants to kill me, it's certain, maybe to share my wealth with someone else. The future is dark indeed! First the ₦200 which Tahiru owes me, then the thousands and thousands which others owe me, and now to crown everything, the spectre of inflation! Terrible inflation. Oh, how terrible, and galloping at that, to chew away my capital and swallow it all up!

JAMILA: What's that you're saying? What's the answer to my request? These ₦200 you know, aren't going into my pocket. They are for the children, for you, and just a bit for me! There are so many things to buy for a family, to feed it and to keep it going!

MAROWACI: I know, I know. They say that but make quite a bit out of the shopping money to constitute a secret fund. First of all, you spend too much! Follow my example and save. Reduce your expenses to the maximum to spend the minimum!

VOICE: Old skin flint, scrooge, shylock!

MAROWACI: Them again! Don't listen to them, Jamila! If I could cut a kobo into four, I would! Why don't they mint smaller coins? (*seeing his wife bite a huge apple she has taken from her pocket*) So! You're eating an apple! And a huge one! A half or a quarter wouldn't be

	enough for you! My word, your eyes are as big as your stomach! You're a glutton! A compulsive eater!
JAMILA:	(*Her mouth full*) Do you want one? (*taking another apple from her pocket*) This one's small, will it be enough for you?
MAROWACI:	Are you mad, or what? Me eat? An apple imported from Europe or America, which must cost more than I earn in a day!
VOICE:	Rotten liar!
MAROWACI:	(*Sighing*) Oh do be quiet! When there are here so many tasty fruits often ten times cheaper than apples!
JAMILA:	What a fuss over a simple apple!
MAROWACI:	Simple apple! A huge fruit worth at least five or eight or even ten naira.
JAMILA:	Ten! You're exaggerating!
MAROWACI:	Oh go on, you're all as bad as one another, the despicable Tahiru, my debtors, my four sons, my daughter, inflation, and you at the top of the list! (*going up to her as she draws back, scared*) Yes, you at the top of the list! You have all made a pact, I feel it, all of you against me! And why? To undo me

	and to share my property! Vultures that's what you are! The whole lot of you!
VOICE:	And what are you, their leader?
MAROWACI:	(*Pulling a wad of notes from his pocket*) Oh shut up! (*counting them*) Here are your ₦200 (*giving the notes*) and make the best use possible! We're on the verge of bankruptcy, so no more apples. Buy mangoes, guavas, oranges and pawpaw, and choose the smallest! Wife, o wife do you understand?
JAMILA:	(*Head down*) Yes, husband! Yes oga sir!
MAROWACI:	Everything I've said has sunk into your little head?
JAMILA:	Yes, husband!
MAROWACI:	So go and attend to your business while I get on with my work!
JAMILA:	(*Going to the door*) Yes Sir (*to the wings*). That was hard, but at least I got my ₦200. But good Lord what have I done to deserve such a husband? (*she goes out*).
MAROWACI:	(*Telephone rings, going to the phone*) Who can that be? Another scrounger probably. Hello! Who is it? Ah, you my cousin! How are you? Fine! Business? Not too good! I'm

hard up, no, I'm not exaggerating... Not at all! So what can I do for you? What? Lend you my car? (*pulls indignant faces and makes gestures showing anger*) I would love to but it's broken down! Ah, you could mend it! I doubt it, since the engine's dead! Yes, dead! Beyond repair! Oh no! Good only for the scrap-yard! I'm sorry cousin, goodbye, see you soon! (*putting the receiver down*) That's all I needed! Borrow my car, brand new, when I run a tax service to make ends meet! Anyway, I loathe the very idea of someone borrowing my car! Well, it's well known, isn't it (*laughing*). There are two things you don't lend – your wife and your car!

Who's that coming? Certainly a client for a loan! He'll be sorry, for I'm obliged to put up my terms because of inflation! I must protect the tool of my trade, and what is that other than the capital I invest in these loans, often money down the drain! So from now on I'll have to charge 150% - 120½% a month, 3% a week or 0.4% a day!

BORROWER: (*Who has arrived*) I'm looking for Mr Marowaci, the moneylender.

MAROWACI: (*Pretending not to have understood*) Pardon me!

BORROWER: I said I was looking for the moneylender, the usurer...

MAROWACI: The usurer, you said?

BORROWER: Yes, the one who lends money out at extortionate rates!

A VOICE: That's him!

MAROWACI: Well here I am!

BORROWER: (*Embarrassed*) You!

MAROWACI: That's me! (*to the wings*) He'll pay all the more since he accuses me of being a usurer, charging extortionate rates!

BORROWER: (*Flustered*) It's about a loan, Mr Marowaci.

MAROWACI: A loan? Do you know that loans in a troubled time like this have a very high interest rate, very high indeed! Some men are charging 200 per cent.

BORROWER: 200%!

MAROWACI: Yes, 200% and it'll probably go up!

BORROWER: Go up!

MAROWACI: Yes, because of inflation! But I can still lend you money at 180%, the rate for friends, of course!

A VOICE:	Friends my eyes!
BORROWER:	Yes, of course! 20% cheaper, that's not bad!
MAROWACI:	And what is the size of the loan you need?
BORROWER:	(*Humbly, eyes down*) ₦50,000, Mr Marowaci.
MAROWACI:	(*Shouting*) ₦50,000! That's a lot, an enormous sum in fact! What is your guarantee?
BORROWER:	A house, and 600 square metres of land.
MAROWACI:	(*Rubbing his hands behind the borrower's back*) That's not much! But I'm generous and kind so I'll accept. Give me your title deeds, my lawyer 'll do the necessary things to legalise the loan and take the guarantee of your house and land. As soon as I have them, I'll give you your ₦50,000.
BORROWER:	Thank you, Mr Marowaci, thanks a lot. (*Aside*) A loan at 180% instead of 200% doesn't happen every day, I'll save 10,000 a year!
A VOICE:	Poor chap, he couldn't be more mistaken!
BORROWER:	(*Aloud*) Goodbye sir (*going to the door*). I'll be here tomorrow at the same time!

MAROWACI: Yes, with the documents.

BORROWER: Indeed (*he goes*).

MAROWACI: That's a good deal! 30% more than 150% that's an extra ₦15,000 per year (*doing sums in his head and making odd gestures*). Oh goodness, I can't work it out. Anyway, the deal is good and will surely increase my capital. That's too much for my grey matter and the figures are so high that it hurts my brain as if there were dust in the mechanism. Oh, my head! Oh my safe - my safes I should say, it's not one safe I have, but ten, or even thirteen! (*laughing*) Thirteen to the dozen, as they say in the market! (*shouting*) See my eggs, thirteen to the dozen for ₦5! Idiot! How could anyone get rich with such customs! Eleven to the dozen would be more like it! And that's what I would say! (*seeing one of his sons arrive*) What does the brat want! Something from me, of course!

A VOICE: Of course!

MAROWACI: My sons! That's the only time I see them! Cadge, cadge! That's what they're best at and the verb they know best, in any form, especially the imperative, cadge, let's cadge they say, according to whether they're alone or in groups. But let's see what this one wants. Number three, I think.

BUKAR:	Hello, Dad.
MAROWACI:	(*Aside*) Yes, no. Three, that's the one (*aloud*) Hello, son! What wind blows you in? A wind of wisdom and economy, I hope!
BUKAR:	(*To the wings*) Wisdom! Economy! So he's going to start his sermon again! How does he expect a young man to survive in this day and age with all the temptations offered? And I, who haven't a kobo in my pocket, what can I do? What should I do? If not ask father for money!
MAROWACI:	You're very quiet! (*aside*) He's probably working out the astronomical sum he is to ask for (*aloud*). Out with it! What wind is it that blows you here?
BUKAR:	A violent wind, father! A real gale, even a hurricane!
MAROWACI:	(*Aside*) He must want a lot to use such words (*aloud*). Well?
BUKAR:	Father, I'm broke... stone broke! I've no pocket money left!
MAROWACI:	(*Interrupting*) No pocket-money left! I curse whoever thought of putting pockets in your clothes! No pockets... No money! I'm going to tell your mother to sew up all your pockets in your jackets and trousers!

BUKAR: You're teasing me, Dad!

MAROWACI: (*Furious*) Me teasing? I couldn't be more serious! What's more, you'll not get another kobo from me, do you hear? No more money for pockets or anything else!

BUKAR: That's cruelty, Dad! How can I live without pocket-money? Do you want me to beg or steal in order to survive?

MAROWACI: (*Imitating him and pulling faces*) How can I survive without pocket money? How can I live without pocket money? Do I have any pocket-money? Me your father, tell me!

BUKAR: You, father, have plain simple money... and lots of it! All the town talks about it. You earn more than most. Your pockets bulge with money.

MAROWACI: All the town talks about it!... and what do they say? (*turning out his pocket*) See what's there in my pocket. A plain cipher!

BUKAR: Shall I also look into your purses, bags and safes?

MAROWACI: You can look over the whole town. But spare me your prying eyes.

BUKAR: Can I say all my ears have heard? If my eyes cannot see what they will?

MAROWACI: Go on! Go on!

BUKAR: You won't get mad at me?

MAROWACI: Go on! I am mad already! Go on!

BUKAR: But...

MAROWACI: But what?

BUKAR: I'm afraid!

MAROWACI: Afraid?

BUKAR: Afraid of a thrashing!

MAROWACI: I shan't touch you! Don't be scared! Come out with all you have to say!

BUKAR: Swear you won't hurt me!

MAROWACI: I swear to you, now. Get on with it! Let me see the dirt of the dirty minds.

BUKAR: They can't be gossiping without reason.

MAROWACI: Then you must be one of them. Go on!

BUKAR: Well they are all in agreement...

MAROWACI: All?

BUKAR: Yes, the whole town!

MAROWACI: Including you I suppose! Go on, I'm listening!

BUKAR: They all agree that you're the wealthiest man in town and even in the province and that your fortune is so great and varied that without the help of several inventory books you cannot even assess your wealth!

MAROWACI: Me, the richest man in the province! Me, the keeper of inventory books. What nonsense! A load of rubbish! There are really people who say that?

BUKAR: All the people in town!

MAROWACI: What else do they say?

BUKAR: That you are the biggest usurer and the greatest skin flint of all time and that Shylock and Scrooge, well-known misers, were nothing as compared to you!

MAROWACI: (*Aside*) I'm getting annoyed indeed! (*aloud*) And these are people of the town? Who says that? Give me an example! Furnish an instance!

BUKAR: Not one, two, three or four of them. But all without exception!

MAROWACI: (*Angry*) Indeed! They shall pay for it.

BUKAR: They say that you ration your wife, daughter, sons, father, mother, servants

	and friends and that people leave your house hungrier than when they went in!
MAROWACI:	Scoundrels! Rascals! Liars!
BUKAR:	That's not all! They say that nothing comes out of your house except smoke from the chimney when you burn your rubbish!
MAROWACI:	Villains! Crows! Rats!
BUKAR:	They defy even a rag-and-bone man to find anything amidst the rubbish you throw out!
MAROWACI:	Liars all!
BUKAR:	That you run an illegal taxi service to pick up a few extra naira! Which is harmful to the poor taxi-drivers already short of work!
MAROWACI:	Villains!
BUKAR:	That in church during the offering, you put buttons and metal discs in the collection plate and that you do the same with the beggars standing outside. That many have heard you mutter that God will pardon you since you are so poor!
MAROWACI:	What liars!

BUKAR:	That you have beaten your wife, my mother, several times since she gave you four sons and only one daughter as it costs more to educate boys than girls. Furthermore, you can marry girls off pretty early and pick up a good dowry!
MAROWACI:	Liars! Bandits!
BUKAR:	I could tell you many similar things till the cows come home. For instance, that you water down the milk and palm wine to make it go further!
MAROWACI:	Liars and scoundrels! I shall have to punish them all! (*taking a stick and hitting his son*) Scoundrels! Villains!
BUKAR:	(*Trying to dodge the blows*) Father! You promised! You swore you wouldn't beat me!
MAROWACI:	It's not you I'm beating, my son, it's them, them I'm beating, punishing, the people of the town!
BUKAR:	Father, maybe in your mind it's them you're hitting. In fact it's me that is getting a sound beating and will be covered with bruises in the end (*aside*). Better to leave I guess, even with empty hands. Let him thrash the air and come back to his senses! (*He runs away*) What would he have done to me if I'd told

him his name Marowaci is synonymous with miserliness!

MAROWACI: So you escape, all of you, liars, scoundrels, villains. Well, every dog has his day! Now here's my daughter coming to me. Is she coming to scrounge or to give me something? It's incredible how my relations with my fellow men are always one way! They always want something, asking, begging, demanding, scrounging, and its always me giving money or help, never the other way round! Yet my greatest pleasure is to receive, not to give! (*To his daughter*) Hello, Binta... I... I'm happy to see you.

BINTA: Hello, Dad, I'm happy too (*aside*) And I'll be even happier, if he gives me what I want!

MAROWACI: (*Aside*) She is growing more beautiful every day, my daughter! I can see two little globes emerging from under her dresses! It's a good sign! Another six months, a year at the most, and... (*smiling*) a good dowry for me! (*to Binta*) So, my little girl, what wind brings you here?

BINTA: (*Playful*) A sweet, gentle breeze, my little daddy (*saucy*) I've brought you a little present daddy... you'll see.

MAROWACI: (*Aside*) A present! A present, even a small one, when I hear of it, it's as if a warning bell rings inside me! Suddenly, I see red, reacting against an unnecessary expense. But well the present is for me! Yet any present from my own family indicates pointless spending, which must eat away my capital, and my capital is sacred! (*Aloud*) A present my dear, for your daddy?

BINTA: Yes, dear daddy, and I hope you'll appreciate it! (*aside*) and that it will prepare him to grant my request!

MAROWACI: Appreciate it? Of course I shall! (*aside*) But of course this present is only part of a game to get something out of me! How cunning, crafty, women can be, they can all put on a sweet act when they have to! But I too can play at that game, and I'll beat her at it pretending I have urgent business to attend to!

BINTA: Here, my little daddy! (*giving the present*).

MAROWACI: (*Taking*) Oh, how kind of you! (*kissing her*) I see my little girl is always thinking of her daddy! But I'll open the parcel later, because I've business to see to now! See you later, dear!

BINTA: But, daddy, I've ...

MAROWACI:	(*Striding away*) See you later, dear! (*to the wings*) The things I have to do to protect my capital!
BINTA:	(*Alone, sighing*) Defeated again! I don't know if I can play the same again! O what we have to do to get our rights! What cunning tricks! What forced smiles! What low-down kowtowing! All to force a man who is my own father to remember his duties! Poor man stricken with such miserliness, that he's no longer a man, but a wall and what a solid wall against any encroachments on his capital.
VOICE:	Poor man indeed!

(*The curtain falls*)

SCENE II

(*The curtain rises, a bedroom where Marowaci keeps his money. A table. A chair. An enormous safe*).

MAROWACI: (*Studying the safe*) This is one of my thirteen safes. It's near them with their treasures, that I feel at my brightest! That I can live at last normally, feeling reborn with my heart opening up, becoming myself!

VOICE: There you surrender your various masks showing your true face of an unrepentant miser, a sordid usurer, a Shylock doubling as a Scrooge.

MAROWACI: That's it! They are back again! The rascals!

ANOTHER VOICE: Back only to throw up the facts at your face!

MAROWACI: (*Towards the voice*) Silence, please, silence, don't interrupt...

VOICE: In the adoration of the golden calf like the Jews at the foot of Mt Sinai! Transformed in your case into an iron safe stuffed with banknotes!

MAROWACI: Whoever you are, wherever you are, leave me in peace, here in my quiet retreat.

VOICE: Good! Pray! Adore, venerate money your God, but don't complain on judgment day when you are straightaway condemned to hell.

MAROWACI: (*Motionless*) (*silence*) Peace at last! (*opening the safe three-quarter full of bank notes*) O my jewels, my friends, my mistresses! (*Grabbing a wad and hugging it*). My mistresses who won't deceive me! Herewith I bring you company! (*revealing a bagful on the ground*) Here are ₦50,000 more naira, 25 piles of banknotes to join you! (*taking them from the bag and looking at them*) This is the delicious fruit of tremendous labour and suffering. First, the pain of earning them, then that of keeping them, repelling incessant attacks by all the would-be sharers, ready to appropriate other people's wealth. Oh, my dear notes! (*Hugging the piles of notes and arranging them in the safe*) I love you, you are the very reason and foundation of my joyous existence! (*Looking a last time at the safe with admiration*) Operation completed!

VOICE: Adoration, more likely!

MAROWACI: And I've twelve more like yourself, o my

golden calf! Full right to the top! In a few days I'll have a 14th delivered. I'll be the only one that will know its destination, or I'll have a constant procession of thieves after it! Thirteen safes, full, and soon fourteen. What happiness! What joy! Each day I visit one. But on Sunday all the thirteen! It's a feast day for me. I get such immense pleasure from contemplating these treasures so well-protected in thirteen metal cases. On such days, I shave well, have a perfumed bath and put on the best of clothes! Once near these treasures I speak softly to them, calling each by its name, having named them all! I open them, to gaze in wonder at the beautiful tidy piles of notes! (*noise outside*) What's happening? I hear voices nearby.

(*Anxiously*) Could I have been spied on and followed! By a cadger? A beggar? A thief? There must be at least two of them, since I hear voices (*scared)* Thieves, they're thieves! A cadger or a beggar would have come alone! Quickly, let me close the safe. Let me draw the curtain which hides it, and put on a placid air, looking serene. (*The two men burst in, holding a gun each*).

BANDIT I: Hands up! Quick! Now where's the money?

MAROWACI: What money?

BANDIT II:	Don't act innocent. We saw you come in with a full bag!
MAROWACI:	You've got the wrong person! Had I come in with a full bag, it would still be here, full or empty!
BANDIT I:	Come on mate. Ransack the room! Carry out a search.
BANDIT II:	Yes, chief, right away (*pulling the curtain*). Simple! The money's in this safe!
BANDIT I:	What a huge safe! If it's full of notes as it should be then we'll be rich indeed!
BANDIT II:	Oh yes, chief, very rich! We shall have enough for the rest of our lives.
BANDIT I:	As for you, you're not smart enough, your camouflage isn't good enough!
MAROWACI:	A good camouflage would have been so expensive! As to the safe don't take it away! I beg! What will you do with a safe?
BANDIT I:	Well, sir, skimping on the camouflage of a safe is unthinkable! But who's taking away the safe! Open it and let's see what there is to take away. Don't take us for fools, hurry up or ...

MAROWACI:	You are the fools! There is no economy you should know that! How do you think I've filled my safes! Er... safe!
BANDIT I:	Safes! So you have many! We'll see to them all don't worry. Open up this one first.
MAROWACI:	Only one, my lords! A slip of the tongue.
BANDIT I:	Be it a slip of the tongue! Open this safe! We shall not carry it away, only the light load inside!
MAROWACI:	(*Kneeling*) Oh no! Don't do that! Take pity! (*Crying*) That's all I have in the world! What's in the safe is my very life!
BANDIT I:	Give me the key if you can't bring yourself to open it! Come on!
MAROWACI:	I can't do that! I can't do that!
BANDIT I:	We'll do it by force then! Come on Bob, search him.
BANDIT II:	(*Jumping on Marowaci, shaking him and rummaging for the keys*) Here they are! (*Waving them*) These are the keys to our fortune!
MAROWACI:	(*Still kneeling*) They're killing me! Taking my life! Murdering me! What use am I

	without my treasure! (*he continues to cry and exclaim all through the scene*).
BANDIT I:	(*To his colleague*) Aim at him while I open the safe!
BANDIT II:	He can do no harm! All he can do is cry!
BANDIT I:	All the same, keep the gun on him, you never know! (*dealing with the safe-lock*) That got it. I've sorted out the combination and (*bursting into laughter*) and... I've opened the safe! A fortune for us!
BANDIT II:	There's a hell of a lot in there!
MAROWACI:	(*Still kneeling and muttering*)
BANDIT I:	(*Looking at Marowaci*) I don't know what you're crying about. It makes no sense! All we want is your money, not your life! You're off your rocker! As for what's in the safe, I'll tell you straight away. (*Making a rapid estimate*) at least a million naira! Go, my mate, and get the bags, quickly, five will do!
BANDIT II:	I'm going! Five, you say?
BANDIT I:	Yes, five (*to Marowaci*). What's wrong with you? You're still alive after all! Anyone else

would have shot you... you won't have this money any more, it's true, but you'll be getting more, and still more. Anyway making money as you do just to admire or adore...

MAROWACI: (*Interrupting*) To adore! I worship it as my god! Don't touch it, leave it alone.

BANDIT I: It is unhealthy! It's a form of madness!

MAROWACI: (*Ecstactically*) I have put all my strength at its service, like a priest, I cannot part with it. Have mercy!

BANDIT I: We're stealing just this million from you! If you have more, hide it better than this. Others much worse could get interested and turn you into a pauper.

MAROWACI: You're torturing me! I can live no more.

BANDIT I: We're being merciful. If only you could see.

BANDIT II: (*Who returns with five bags and hands over one to Marowaci*) Go on! Get on with it! You've stacked them! Now it's up to you to get them out!

MAROWACI: (*Groaning and pulling faces*) It gives me more pain to get them out than pleasure

	to stack them in. It's a terrible punishment. (*Taking out the piles slowly one by one*) Worse than the most painful torture. Oh my poor dears, now orphaned! What shall I do?
BANDIT I:	(*Pushing Marowaci aside*) Go on. Let's get on with it. Or we'll still be here in a week!
BANDIT II:	(*Filling bags quickly along with his mate, under Marowaci's sad face*) It hurts him to see them come out of the safe, but it's just the opposite for us!
BANDIT I:	One man's meat...
BANDIT II:	Is another man's poison!
BANDIT I:	(*Taking out the last pile*) That's it! A full million! All's well!
BANDIT II:	(*Estactic*) We're rich!
BANDIT I:	At least on the point of being rich! But we'd better get out of here. Take the bags! I'll carry two. You do the same (*to Marowaci*). And you take the last! Let's all go, men and bags (*to Marowaci*). We'll dump you in the countryside... and we'll get away with the five bags, pleased to have met you.

MAROWACI: You want me to take my life with my own hands!

BANDIT I: You'll soon have more money! And that's your life! Your state of being an orphan won't last long! You're an expert in the art of making money and of stashing it away, a fanatic hoarder of money. Your name Marowaci means miser and thief throughout the province! The news of your fame has reached us and we're not even from your province!

MAROWACI: It reached you?

BANDIT I: Yes, and now let's move! A word of advice! Don't come back here. It'll upset you. (*They all leave, dragging the bags, as the curtain falls*).

SCENE III

MAROWACI: (*Sadly looking at the empty safe*) I'm a widower, a divorcee, an orphan all at the same time! Mourning for a million passed into the hands of strangers. O but let me not cry on because I've other twelve, filled up. Let me rather improve upon the aspect of security and think about the surest way of recuperating the million. First I'll cut down on spending. Tightening our belts is the first thing all of us, wife, daughter, sons have to do, and I'll set the example! The second thing to do is to add to income as such as possible. The surest way is to put up the interest rate. From 180%, I'll go up to 200% per annum, 16.66% per month, 3.80% a week and 0.548% a day!

VOICE: Marowaci, you're incorrigible, you miser and usurer for all time to come.

MAROWACI: (*Laughing*) Voice! Whoever you are, wherever you come from, leave me in peace, at least now! I've enough problems on my hand without you! Let them come now, sons and daughter, to scrounge for pocket money and I'll show them the way out! Mother come begging for housekeeping money and she'll find the door shut, or rather I'll slam it in her face!

	A sudden thought! I can save a lot on clothes! Shorts use less material than trousers! That's it! Shorts for the boys still they're twenty! As for my daughter she'll wear miniskirts till she's married, even if they're out of date. They cost half the price of a long dress!
VOICE:	Miniskirts... Binta! Oh good, what a view we'll get!
MAROWACI:	Them again! Vermin! Well, let no one here throw money out of the windows. Better to shut or block up the windows. Another way of saving is to inspire pity. A look of poverty puts off scroungers! I'll follow the rule: never show you're rich. Wear worn-out clothes, even patched ones! Don't be afraid to show your arse in the interest of wearing a look of poverty. And now (*Puffing himself up*). Let them come: borrowers, gangsters, wife, children, daughter or sons, and any other parasites! I'm ready for them, more than ever!

(*The Curtain Falls*)

ENVY

PROLOGUE

CAST:

HENRY PETERS: Envy - 55 years, very lean and sulky looking.

RITA PETERS: His wife - 45 years, plump, pretty and always smiling.

ROBERT MORRIS: Ever successful. 45 years, handsome, sure of himself.

EVELYN MORRIS: His wife. Very pretty. 40 years. Up-to-date in her fashions as well as information

PRESENTER
MISER
ENVIOUS PERSON

The presenter enters. Thirteen characters are lined up on the right hand side of the stage. A notice round their necks indicates which deadly sin each one represents. Eleven of them are mannequins, two are human beings. These last two represent avarice and envy respectively.

PRESENTER: (*Pointing with the stick she's holding at the person representing avarice*) Take a good look at the sad person here representing avarice. He's indeed a wretched creature, a dried-up body and heart, quite consumed by his excessive love for money. Take yourself off! Clear off, you miser! (*she hits him with the stick*) Out! We've had enough of your horrid presence. Go on! Off with you! (*she chases him*) Double quick, you owl!

MISER: (*Tearfully, fleeing, filled with shame*) Have mercy! Don't hit me! I'm off!

PRESENTER: And now let's behold the attendant of these men, the sixth, (*counting on his fingers*), yes, the sixth (*she goes towards the one representing envy, takes him by the hand and pulls him in front of her and announces in a loud voice*). Ladies and gentlemen, here is Envy that would smite you all.

ENVY: (*Bowing to the audience*) Ladies and gentlemen, I am indeed her! (*running, pirouetting and doing a couple of somersaults*) I am envious, indeed! Envy personified in all it's sinful splendour and elevated state! I envy the very heat of the sun, the very light of the stars, the very pallor of the moon (*pirouettes*). I envy all and everything, men, the beasts, kings, emperors, leaders of every creed, be they democrats, plutocrats, theocrats or autocrats, big or small, weak or strong! (*somersaults*) I envy the ruthless strength of the lion, the unwitting perfidy of the serpent, the swift, irresistible flight of the eagle! I envy my own neighbours, father, mother, sisters, brothers, children, in a word, everything and everyone in the universe, indeed in all other universes! (*stages a final pirouette and two somersaults*) Envy I am and shall remain! (*he disappears*).

(*The curtain falls*).

ACT I
SCENE I

(The Peters' sitting room, indifferently furnished, in poor taste).

RITA: I'm happy Henry, and proud of you. We've achieved our goal. At last we have a pretty house and...

HENRY: (*Interrupting*) A pretty house! (*to the wings*) Talk about a pretty house! A pretty house with only one floor, when the Morrises have three floors! (*To Rita*) A nice house, if you say? Maybe!

RITA: Anyway it's a nice house. We've two nice cars too!

HENRY: Two nice cars?

RITA: A Peugeot 504, and the 105 I use!

HENRY: Well, it's true of course we have a 504 SR and a 105! (*to the wings and almost shouting*) But, good grief! What's a 504 SR and a 105 in comparison to a 605 GL and a 505 SR which the Morisses have! That damned Morris, I'm always a few models behind him! Imagine me driving a model inferior to his wife's! That's what gets me down most of the time, and gets on my nerves. It's as if Morris is permanently making fun of me. I'm sure he's making a fool of me, always raising the bar just as I'm about to reach it. Two years ago he was driving a 504 SR and his wife a 105 while I had to make do with a 104 and my wife with buses and taxis! And tomorrow, when I struggle to his level, my head just above the waves and my tongue hanging out, he has put the bar even higher. And how far will he go? Maybe one day he'll start on racing cars and collector's cars, unless... unless he turns his thoughts to flying machines!

RITA: Henry, what's the matter with you? Are you dreaming or what? Gesticulating right under my nose! As if I weren't there at all!

HENRY: Oh, leave me alone! There's nothing the matter! I'm thinking, that's all. About one thing only.

RITA: And what might this thing be? If I may know.

HENRY: That times are hard. When you think you've found happiness, it flies away like a WILL-O-THE WISP!

RITA: Henry, old chap, are we not happy? Tell me!

HENRY: (*Raising his voice*) Happiness, what happiness! What is your happiness? Tell me that!

RITA: Just what I said earlier! Our house, our two cars, and our two bank accounts here in Lagos and those we have in London and Geneva!

HENRY: Don't tell anyone about them! Don't forget it's not legal to have them! They are as good as not there. You know too much! You speak too much!

RITA: Not very legal, I quite agree. But tell me, who hasn't got such accounts? Even the top men have them!

HENRY: Of course! Of course! Whether they're top men in politics or business! The higher in fact they are, the fatter the accounts. But keep that to yourself. Don't go and shout it out from the rooftops, or you'll find yourself out on your ears, living on millet, yam and water with only rats, lizards, spiders and mosquitoes for company.

RITA: How awful! Rats, lizards and spiders! In spite of the house we have!

HENRY: Quite right! Quite right! If only you knew. These bigwigs, believe me, have accounts hundred times as big as ours! (*aside his face twisted with envy*) They count dollars by the million, I count them by the hundred. I have a powerful urge, a terrible urge, to rid the world of such people, so that I may be number one in everything! Ah, Envy! It's my biggest vice and greatest strength, by far! I can't bear anyone to have more than me. When anyone is seen to have more, a feeling of irritation, even hatred arises in me! Then I change colour, blood rushes to my head, insults to my mouth, lightning to my eyes... and mustard to my nose! (*to his wife*) Yes, my dearest! The big-shots who are heads above me make me feel like a dwarf, and it makes me suffer, terribly! (*agitated*) Such a situation is simply intolerable! To be a dwarf among giants is nothing to shout about and not at all enviable! Why must I be grovelling under someone's heel. I curse the heavens that are against me, always putting me in second place, when I've got it in me to be in first.

RITA: Henry, my dear, can't you be content with what you have? Why not take a look beneath for a change? You look up enough to unscrew your neck, raising yourself on your toes to get a better look at the giants. For once, why not look at the dwarfs, that is, those smaller than yourself!

HENRY: You're asking for the impossible. I must be up not down.

RITA: Listen! Everything is relative in this mean world. So content yourself with what you have. Contentment after all is great wealth.

HENRY: Content myself? Me? Me, Henry Peters! Never! "Always higher and higher" is my motto! I'll always envy someone that's my nature! My divine nature.

RITA: Henry, there's a limit to everything! Can you for example go higher than the vault of heaven?

HENRY: Well, my dear, you're a thousand years behind time. You haven't even reached Ptolemy, who, poor chap, placed the earth at the centre of the universe! You should know there are millions of systems similar to our solar system! And so there's no end to going higher and higher.

RITA: Sorry, Henry, I admit my ignorance. Millions? You really mean millions? And you can always go higher and higher?

HENRY: Yes, millions, in fact, billions, if you must know. And there's no limit to reaching higher. None!

RITA: Does that make the sun jealous? That it is not the biggest body in space?

HENRY: The spots and explosions on its surface may well be fits of envy, anger and indignation!

RITA: Come back to earth, Henry. Let's leave the stars to their courses that we understand but little. I maintain that we, you and I, can live happily as we are. We've all we need to do so. For example, the son we love is in his third year at University of Lagos and our daughter in first year at University of Maiduguri, whereas so many children never get beyond primary school!

HENRY: Unilag, Unimaid, Unical, UI whatever you wish! It isn't worth tuppence! Secondary schools in disguise with the pompous names of university, that's what they are! Morris' children are studying abroad in institutions of great fame! Do you realise? One of the twins is in GB the other in USA, a third son in Ireland and their daughter in France!

RITA: (*Admiringly*) In France?

HENRY: Yes, in France! What do you think? So tell me, how can I not be envious of such a situation. It is simply unjust? (*walking up and down*) Truly, I curse the heavens. If some people are born under a lucky star, I wasn't born under any star at all. Perhaps I was born under the waning moon, not even a full moon. Just a little scrap of pale moon, a puny little scrap I must have been born under! And you want me to be content!

RITA: Henry dear! How can you curse heaven and insult the moon?

HENRY: Do not the Morrises and others like them make fun of me? Tell me that!

RITA: I don't believe it! They get on with their work and do as well as they can! What can they get out of making fun of you and me!

HENRY: Oh, you're always happy! I admire you, my dear, and envy you! You see, I'm always envying someone, and now it's you! It's a chronic ailment with me I know, I've always been like that! As a little boy I never touched what was on my own plate, always wanting what was on my brother's plate, thinking it was better. So that's what I am. And that's how I wish to be!

RITA: Two dogs reared together act in the same way, one trying to eat out of the other's dish.

HENRY: Oh, so you're comparing me to a dog now! Thanks a lot! At least you're not envious, happy with a man who behaves like a dog! But take care, one day I could well start to bark and bite!

RITA: I love you, my little husband, just as you are, with your virtues and vices (*a knock on the door*). Who could that be? (*going towards the door*) I'm not expecting anyone at this time (*she half-opens the door and receives a letter from someone we can't see*). Thanks! Give my best wishes to Mrs Morris.

HENRY: A letter from Mrs Morris?

RITA: Yes, from Mrs Morris.

HENRY: What does she want from us?

RITA: From me, actually. But let me read the letter first.

HENRY: She probably wants to invite you, because she certainly won't go as far as inviting both of us! She knows me too well and has understood that I can't outdo them, the pair of them, man and woman. They are my pet aversion, those people who invite us so that we can admire all they have.

RITA: Oh come on, you're exaggerating! (*beginning to read the letter*) Please do let me read!

HENRY: (*Aside*) My pet aversion? Him, for sure, but her! She's beautiful, the bitch. I envy Morris for having such a pretty, fresh wife while I have an ugly one, so much the worse for wear (*getting roused*) My word! I could have a good time with little Evelyn Morris. Oh yes! No matter where. On cushions, out in the bush or even on the ground if necessary! That woman gives me the urge. Oh goodness, what an urge! I'd give my soul to the devil to satisfy it!

RITA: (*Stops reading*) (*aside*) There we go, he's off with his prayers again! (*out loud*) Henry, what's the matter? Aren't you listening? You never listen!

HENRY: Nothing, my dear, nothing at all. There's absolutely nothing the matter. But I'm irritated thinking about what's in that letter you're holding. She's inviting you for sure, not me, not both.

RITA: How can you be sure it's only me she's inviting?

HENRY: It's damned obvious! She just cannot bear the sight of me for I hate what they are and what they have!

RITA: Well, you're wrong, because you're invited **too**. Moreover here's the invitation which came with the letter. Here, read it if you don't believe me.

HENRY: (*Taking the card*) Mr and Mrs Peters. Well, it's true. I'm certainly invited. What does that mean? It's the first time that's happening to me... ah... to us. Those people have always kept their distance. There must be some trick I tell you!

RITA: Will you accept the invitation? That's the point. There's no end to imagining!

HENRY: I'm not too sure. Everything tells me to refuse, to show those two that I too can wish to keep my distance. On the other hand, something tells me to accept for I'm anxious to know what such an invitation can hide, and also to see what their house is like inside, how they receive their guests, what they eat and drink. In a word, to see how these "giants" I envy so much live!

RITA: I'm glad you'll accept. At last we'll get out of our isolation and associate with people richer and more powerful than ourselves. You ought to be happy to see these people in their own environment. It'll give you ideas about how to improve your chances and your status.

HENRY: It'll certainly make me more envious than ever! (*Aside*) It's especially my desire for the lovely Evelyn, which will become keener, inflating the bird in my trousers. The expression 'bursting with desire' could well apply to me? (*to Rita*) Indeed! When are we invited? I didn't notice.

RITA: Next week Saturday. So we've ten days to get ready.

HENRY: Get ready and polish our language, for we must shine that evening. If you don't shine with your clothes and jewels, it's by your witty word at just the right moments that you'll shine, each word like pearls from your mouth!

RITA: And yours like sapphires and diamonds!

HENRY: Which for once will make them the envious and us the envied (*laughs*).

(*The curtain falls*)

SCENE II

Morrises' drawing room, richly furnished but in bad taste.

ROBERT: (*Singing*) Life is sweet... sweet... sweet. The sheep they bleat... bleat... bleat.

EVELYN: You're very cheerful today! I hope it's not the invitation you've just sent that has made you like that! What's got into you to have made you invite such people, I'd like to know, especially him. I just can't abide him! He's so obnoxious.

ROBERT: Why do you think I've invited him? It's not for his good looks. That's certain! It's only that I may need him for the next elections. To say I'll try to make friends with him means I'll stroke the animal so he'll not bite me!

EVELYN: At the next elections? Whatever for?

ROBERT: The next elections! I'm yet to tell you that I'm going into politics! If I can manipulate Henry Peters he can be very valuable to me! He has a certain influence among his sort! As you have surely noticed, he's so envious. It's hard to understand. So I'll promise to open doors for him to get where I've already reached. In politics you have to be obsequious and know how to flatter, lie, cajole, promise a lot and give but little.

EVELYN: I'll take note, thanks! As for Peters, he's certainly envious. The dose of envy that runs through him is large indeed!

ROBERT: So that he can really play bare, and show his true face, we'll leave them alone, him and his wife, a few moments. Thanks to the two-way mirror and the mike I've installed. We'll be able to follow their actions and expressions and hear his comments, for it will be Peters who'll talk. Theatre, my dear, theatre, and comedy at that, is what you'll see!

EVELYN: I'm sure of it! It's ingenious, your two-way mirror and mike! I have a feeling we're going to have fun. I'm expecting rather interesting commentaries and grimaces and foolery. He is a clever man no doubt. We do need to have a laugh.

ROBERT: Without doubt. If the wife is rather reserved, he, my goodness, has a long tongue and a rapid delivery when fed by his morbid envy. It's quite simple. He's jealous of everyone and I'm quite sure he's as jealous of our Head of State as of the Queen of England, Emperor of Russia or the President of USA, be he a peanut merchant, a second rate actor or whatever you like! (*the door bell rings*) That 'll be them, I bet. Be prepared!

EVELYN: (*Going to the door*) I am!

ROBERT: (*Straightening up*) Me too!

EVELYN: (*Opening the door*) My dear friends! Come in!

ROBERT: (*Approaching*) Yes, come in! You can't imagine how pleased we are to see you. It's your first visit, isn't it?

HENRY: (*Followed by Rita, looking around with a sickly sweet expression*) Yes, the first visit, I think, but wait, (*thinking*) Yes it is the first visit... but still, wait! Unless... oh no, oh yes, it is indeed our first visit. (*To the wings*) As if he didn't know, the dog, that it's the first and only time he's inviting us! He really has a way of showing his contempt. But I'll have my revenge, and soon! And it'll be a devastating revenge! "One often needs someone smaller than oneself," as the saying goes, and the smaller one won't be the one you think!

RITA: Yes, indeed, it's our first visit and my pleasure is all the more for that. It's like a young girl's first ball.

HENRY: And for me, (*laughing*) it has the same effect as doing you know what, has for a young man! (*all laugh*).

ROBERT: Bravo! At least you like a good joke!

HENRY: (*To the wings*) And a good cry, old chap!

EVELYN: You'll be good company!

HENRY: That has been known to happen! (*aside, looking at Evelyn*) Especially when I find myself alone with a bit of stuff like her, near a big soft bed, but certainly not when I compare my poky little house with the unlimited luxury here!

EVELYN: You'll have to excuse me a moment. Our staff have their day off today, so we'll have to lend a hand.

ROBERT: That 'll be more friendly and cosy.

EVELYN: And you can't say what you like in front of servants!

HENRY: That's quite true (*to the wings*). Lucky for those who have servants! As for me, apart from my two arms and two legs and damn all else, I have nothing to play the part of a valet! (*looking ferocious*) But that 'll change! It has to! Oh yes! One way or another! (*addressing Robert*) That's absolutely true! There's no one more talkative than a servant, more likely to spread gossip and tittle-tattle.

EVELYN: (*Going towards the pantry followed by Robert*) Will be back in a moment. We haven't much to do.

HENRY: (*To Robert who's closing the door*) See you in a tic (*the Morrises go behind what is supposedly the two-*

way mirror, which separates the drawing room from the kitchen).

ROBERT: You see, Evelyn, behind the two-way mirror, we can see without being seen, and we can hear without being heard, thanks to the mike. So now, take your seat in the theatre.

HENRY: The field is clear... Let's make the most of it (*Prancing around the room and pirouetting).* Make the most of it, have a look at all these marvels... Well, so-called marvels. The furniture's not worth much. Imitations, copies of Louis... IXX.. no, not quite... Louis XVII style! Ah, dammit... doesn't matter, it's Louis something! (*dashing over to a black wooden statue and picking it up to weigh it*) that's ebony, I'll be bound (*weighing a second one, then another*) Well, these two are fakes, vulgar white wood painted black or varnished. They must have bought that in the flea market or the thieves' market.

ROBERT: (*To Evelyn*) What did I tell you, darling! Theatre! More theatre! Always theatre!

EVELYN: And without being seen! Watching freely someone who thinks he's alone, spouting out whatever's on his mind!

ROBERT: A load of twaddle, that's what's on his mind, if he has one! Quiet! Let's look and listen!

RITA: (*To Henry, who's feeling and weighing a corner of the carpet*) Henry, you're going too far! If they could see and hear you!

HENRY: No chance of that, there's the great wall of China between us! And so what if they did see or hear me? Would they make me a hole when I've already got one? Tell me! (*muted laughs from the Morrises*) What is it? Who's laughing?

RITA: Oh nothing! The Morrises must be having fun behind the great wall of China as you call it.

ROBERT: (*Signalling to Evelyn to be quiet*) Sh! We'd better not laugh so loud.

HENRY: Let them enjoy themselves! He who laughs last laughs loudest! In any case these carpets are rubbish, believe me, it's industrial carpet! I promise you, Rita, that when we get carpets for our house, it'll be decent quality and handmade at that!

RITA: You can always dream! At least they've got a carpet! As for us...

HENRY: So you have no faith in me, and you say that aloud! If they heard and saw you, do you realise how insulting it would be?

RITA: There's the great wall of China between us, don't forget!

HENRY: Walls have ears sometimes! (*Morrises laughing*) The Morrises again? They must be laughing very loud, if we can hear them unless their walls are wafer thin, which wouldn't surprise me in the least! It's a shack, this house and I don't know why I should be jealous of such a hut!

ROBERT: (*Tapping Evelyn's arm*) Do you hear that?

HENRY: My dear Rita, I promise you a house that 'll be a real house, carpets, statues, wall-hangings, paintings and fabulous furniture, everything better than here!

RITA: Have you seen their furniture?

HENRY: And as well as that, I promise we'll rise in society, higher than... higher than this punch, if I have to walk over his dead body!

EVELYN: Punch! The lowdown so-and-so! He's going too far!

ROBERT: Leave it! He is a force to channel, a puppet to manipulate!

RITA: Henry, I've taken note of your good intentions, but have you seen their furniture? Have you had a good look!

HENRY: Well, what's better about their furniture than any other?

RITA: But it's really beautiful!

HENRY: Beautiful? That old junk? You'll always make me laugh Rita!

RITA: Junk may be, but junk that we don't possess!

HENRY: I'd rather you shut up or I'll get angry and we'll come to blows. Moreover, I hear noise, it'll be the Morrises coming back, let's be quiet! (*the Morrises come out from behind the two-way mirror*).

ROBERT: (*Appearing in the door way*) Hi! We're back.

EVELYN: I hope you weren't bored. Sorry!

HENRY: Bored? Us? Not at all. We were admiring all your lovely things, they are such treasures!

EVELYN: Oh, you think so?

HENRY: Certainly, We've never seen such lovely things, isn't that so, Rita?

RITA: Oh yes! Everything is superb.

ROBERT: Good! (*aside*) Bloody liar! All he's done is criticise everything he has seen!

HENRY: Oh yes, everything's superb and of the best taste.

ROBERT: (*To the wings*) Just the man I need, intelligent, crafty, artful, capable of blatant lies, flattery, and completely obsequious and servile, servant and master all in one! (*to Henry*) Thanks, thanks, my dear friend, I feel we can get along very well and have a warm friendship.

HENRY: (*Hand on his heart*) I hope so, wholeheartedly, and I hope it will happen quickly (*to the wings*) Here's someone who needs me, but to what cunning end? What shady purpose? I can't imagine, but for whatever reason, I'll make him pay through the nose for my services! Moreover, what I want most of all is to depose him and take his place, whatever and wherever that is!

ROBERT: If you like, we'll do the tour of the two floors.

RITA: Oh, with pleasures! (*aside*) That way my husband 'll know what to do to keep his promise and give me as beautiful a house as this! What am I saying? More beautiful!

HENRY: (*Who wants to be alone with the beautiful Mrs Morris*) You three go on, I've a sore leg so I can't go upstairs.

RITA: Sore leg? (*seeing Henry make eyes at her*) Oh, your arthritis I was forgetting, how silly of me!

ROBERT: So Mrs Peters, if you'd like to follow me, Evelyn

	will keep your husband company. Won't you dear?

EVELYN: Of course, with the greatest of pleasure.

RITA: (*To Robert Morris who's already on the bottom stair*) I'm coming.

HENRY: (*To the wings, making faces*) And me too! With what pleasure I find myself, *tête à tête,* face to face, alone with her! If only it could be more intimate! Oh ouh ah uh... more intimate! Bum to bum! Oh la la! But hang on... Morris and my wife, that old sour-face, will never be far away, and this woman isn't the sort to jump into bed! How beautiful she is, if I compare her to my ugly old bag of a wife! It's like comparing a female monkey to the Venus de Milo! How can one not be envious when one is the victim of such circumstances. My word, it's a trick of heaven which gives plenty to one man and very little to another! And not content with offering material riches to one, luxury cars, a sumptuous home, it gives him a prize pin-up with a madonna's face! (*to Evelyn*) (*Blushing with confusion, and stammering*) My dear, my dear, my dar... my dear, that is my dear friend... make... make... (*after a silence*). I make the most of this chance to express all the admiration I have for you... (*silence*) You are so pretty, it's a pleasure to look at you, to study you like a flower!

EVELYN: Mr Peters, you flatter me too much! I'm not prettier than any one else! Your wife for example (*mocking*) is a great beauty and I come nowhere near her in that respect!

HENRY: My wife? That ugly bag? Don't talk about her! She's more like a scarecrow than anything else!

EVELYN: Mr Peters all the same, you can't talk about your wife like that!

HENRY: She has nothing going for her, poor woman, whereas you have everything, your eyes, lips, breasts! Ah, your breasts! Two little marvels exciting and provoking, and to crown it all, you...

EVELYN: (*Interrupting*) Mr Peters. Pull yourself up, please! (*Aside*) It's going beyond the bounds of decency.

HENRY: Pull myself up! No! (*almost beseeching*) Let me finish telling you all I have to say Evelyn! And your bottom, divided beautifully into two such well-shaped buttocks, fitting nicely in your dress, and such a lovely curve to your legs, and your thighs, Evelyn which hide so well the sacred place where lies the forbidden fruit! Oh Eve! My love! I would like to touch, caress, kiss with my lips every bit of your body and greedily gather the treasure – flower or fruit which you guard so well!

EVELYN:	Mr Peters! Please! Calm down! How can you utter such things when my husband and your wife could hear?
HENRY:	I don't give a damn, Evelyn (*almost shouting*) I love you!
EVELYN:	Oh my God! You're mad! (*aside*) That does it!
HENRY:	Yes, mad! And mad for you! (*aside*) I've never wanted a woman so much! Oh my God! My thing is hard and on fire. It wants only to get out of its cage!
EVELYN:	I know you were envious, but not in this way!
HENRY:	Envy in my case has many facets, and my love for you is one of them, and not the least!
EVELYN:	Henry, stop it or I'll call my husband!
HENRY:	(*Closer to her*) Oh, Eve, my darling! Do you want to ruin a newborn love?
EVELYN:	Yes, nip in the bud a love with no future!
HENRY:	(*Arms round her*) Oh, Eve, just to embrace you, to possess you on this armchair or even on the carpet!
EVELYN:	(*Pushing him off*) Let me go, I beg you!

HENRY: (*Arms round her again*) And conjugate together the verb "to love"!

EVELYN: (*Pushing him away violently and slapping him*) I've never seen in one man so much envy nor a single head full of such folly!

HENRY: (*Holding his cheek*) Nor I a woman with so much sternness and wickedness.

EVELYN: (*Noticing her husband and Mrs Peters returning*) Phew! Saved! (*sarcastic*) Pull yourself together Mr Peters and come back to reality. You've had a dream that's all!

HENRY: (*Rubbing his cheek*) A bit of a mad but beautiful dream!

EVELYN: (*To Henry*) A bit? A lot! (*to her husband*) Ah, dear, I've had a very interesting discussion with Mr Peters. He is full of wit and humour, and really good humour!

HENRY: Oh come on, don't exaggerate! (*aside*) She means love, not humour. She's making fun of me, the sharp customer, and she's not far from wrong! I made myself ridiculous. I realise now, that if ridicule could kill, I'd have died a few times over! How can I overcome Envy, this Envy which possesses me? Which dominates me, which is my master? Envy of other man's wives, cars, houses. I'm afflicted with the worst of vices,

	envy, which makes me permanently dissatisfied, wretched, forcing myself to laugh when I should laugh heartily, who curses what should be applauded, who... who, well who does everything the wrong way round!
ROBERT:	No, Mr Peters. Evelyn isn't exaggerating, it's not her custom. If she say you are full of humour, then you must be! (*quietly to Peters*) And now, my friend, I must discuss with you something of the greatest importance, which requires the utmost discretion (*to the two women*). Ladies, we'll leave you for a little while, for Mr Peters and I have things to discuss.
EVELYN:	(*Feigning surprise*) Yes, well, do so, but be quick, please, Robert, be brief! I wouldn't like to miss a moment of Mr Peter's company, his sense of humour is so outstanding!
HENRY:	(*Aside*) There she goes again making fun of me and I'm the only one to know she's having a go at me! (*to Robert*) Let's go then, I'm all ears! (*aside*) to know how he wants to make use of me, so as to gain something out of it!
ROBERT:	I'll lead the way, excuse me (*they leave together*).
EVELYN:	(*To Rita*) Well, now we're alone. Let's talk woman's talk!
RITA:	We certainly have many things to talk about.

EVELYN: No doubt we have and if you agree I'll start straight away and you'll see fireworks as you have never seen before!

RITA: Fireworks! What do you mean?

EVELYN: Yes fireworks, because your darling of a husband gave me a hard time! He told me such horrible things, oh my God! Horrible enough to make the very devil blush!

RITA: Oh how dreadful! But what has he told you?

EVELYN: My poor lady, if you knew what he said... But I hesitate to repeat all what he has told me!

RITA: But you must! One never knows somebody thoroughly, and I am anxious to discover the hidden face of my dear husband, if there is one!

EVELYN: I am hesitating because I am afraid to sadden you.

RITA: Go on, don't be afraid!

EVELYN: Well in short he has had a very acute fit of envy! Very acute indeed!

RITA: Oh envy! Always the same failing, this fault will be his downfall.

EVELYN: And I was the subject of his envy, imagine! He

wanted me body and soul, rejecting you as one throws away an object which has become useless!

RITA: (*Offended*) O the wretched creature!

EVELYN: Calling you scarecrow and ugly mug without any sex appeal!

RITA: (*Infuriated*) Swine! Old billy-goat! Infamous bastard!

EVELYN: And you can't imagine how difficult it has been to dissuade him from... I'll not say more.

RITA: To dissuade him from what? Tell me!

EVELYN: To force me to have sex with him, there, in the next room, on the carpet, like a beast!

RITA: Bastard! Sex maniac!

EVELYN: But do not repeat a single word of what I have just told you. It's highly confidential you understand? Women must help one another.

RITA: I am and I'll be always ready to practise this mutual aide which will enable us to know our husbands better.

EVELYN: By the way, what about my own husband? Did he make a pass at you?

RITA: Yes he did, at several occasions! But in a less brutal way I must admit! The dear man arranged everything: place, date and time! His sexual desire was there alright and quite visible, that I can swear!

EVELYN: Oh the dirty beast! The traitor! Always ready to fornicate wherever he is!

RITA: But my dear friend all the men are the same! Whether they have beautiful wives or not, they'll always find the neighbour's own nicer!

EVELYN: You are right! What you have just said is the sad truth! Men are rogues! Swines!

RITA: Quite right! But I'll take care of curing my useless husband of the terrible defect he is afflicted with; this defect he has to envy everybody and above all the husbands who have beautiful wives.

EVELYN: What about mine! I'll give him a shock treatment he is not going to forget! O envy! Defect, sickness, so vicious and very often so related to lechery!

RITA: These two deadly sins go hand in hand.

EVELYN: And men are their easy victims!

RITA: Well my dear, this closes the fireworks which you told me about.

EVELYN: Yes... But now remain two other fireworks, yours and mine, which will have as only spectators our respective husbands... ourselves acting as fireworks experts!

RITA: It'll be their turn to see stars!

EVELYN: And many of them!

RITA: To everyone his turn, isn't it?

EVELYN: Rita you are one hundred per cent correct! Their pernicious envy must disappear!

RITA: Before they pass away!

EVELYN: Poor Robert!

RITA: And poor Henry!

EVELYN: Thanks to whom we roar with laughter!

(*The curtain falls*)

PRIDE AND AMBITION OR "THE SUN-KING"

CAST:
KUROMA
KINGSTON
THE SERVANT
THE BARKER
THE INSTRUCTOR
MONICA
COLONEL MANGA (LATER MARSHAL MANGA)

PROLOGUE:

The lady introducer arrives on the scene. Thirteen forms which look like dummies are aligned on the right side of the scene. Three of them are real human beings representing greed, lust and pride.

THE LADY INTRODUCER: (*Indicating with the tip of her stick the actor representing greed*) Dear spectators, you have already seen this unsavoury individual who is Greed. (*She touches him with her stick*). He is a despicable character, very fat and very ugly! Go away Mr Greed, out of here! (*she gives him some strokes of the stick*) clear off! We have seen enough of your abominable plumpness! (*she drives him away in front of her*) Quicker than that! Come on! At the double! Rush off!

MR GREED: (*Runs away crying*) No! Don't beat me! No strokes on my ribs! I'm leaving without waiting to hear more!

THE LADY INTRODUCER: Phew! We had seen enough of that one! You have also seen this horrible character who represents Lust! (*she touches him lightly with her stick*) A very detestable creature. Run away Mr Lust, you who're interested only in the pleasure of the senses (*she drives him out hitting him with her stick*). We have seen enough of your face on which your vice is written so large.

MR LUST: (*Running away without waiting to hear more*) I am going straightaway to meet Cleo... who is my goddess, my priestess... my only aim in life and my philosophy.

THE LADY INTRODUCER: Let's now see the third of these characters! (*she moves towards the actor representing pride and holds him with her hand and pushes him in front of her. Announcing with a loud voice)* Here is the third culprit: Pride and Ambition! (*the actor representing this deadly sin is dressed in clothes embroidered all over with gold and diamonds*).

MR PRIDE: (*Bowing down to the spectators*) Ladies and Gentlemen: Pride and Ambition!

(*The curtain falls*)

ACT I

SCENE I

A big sitting room richly furnished but without refinement. Some luxurious hangings cover the walls. Some thick and soft carpets cover the floor. The room is garnishly lighted by crystal chandeliers. Everything reflects the character nouveau riche, placing the owner in the category of swanks.

The host is seated in a big armchair made of ebony wood inlaid with ivory and precious stones. He is dressed in richly embroidered clothes. Two servants are standing up, arms crossed. One is on his right, the other on his left.

MR KINGSTON: (*Talking to the servant on his left in a scornful tone*) You there, on my left, call my cultural counsellor for me and quickly, eh! But you are dozing, stupid twitt! If you're really interested in keeping this golden position, change your attitude! Do you get me? And now go! Clear off!

THE SERVANT: (*Aloud*) Yes sir... I am flying off, sir... (*going away and speading off*) A golden position, a golden position, let's talk about it! A position at which the owner of the house shoots an insult every second! (*he goes out. Then arrives the counsellor who is also richly dressed*).

KUROMA: (*Content with himself, he coughs to attract the attention of the proud men*) Mr Kingston, how are you? You look an excellent shape today, bright eyes, fresh complexion, a youthful face! How do you manage to remain so youthful? What's your secret! A magical concoction, eh? Extracted from leaves or roots? Some concoction having as a base the grease or blood of a lion, panther or leopard? Come on, let me know!

KINGSTON: Neither roots, nor leaves, nor a magic cure. My dear Kuroma, only the good star under which I was born!

KUROMA: I implore heaven that this good star may protect you for ever!

KINGSTON: Thank you my dear, thank you; but let's turn to something more serious. What's the news, what advice would you give?

KUROMA: Today it's rather poor, all is quiet, and nobody moves. Everybody is lying low! It's because the naira is becoming scarce even when it is worthless!

KINGSTON: Not the smallest piece of advice?

KUROMA: Well, I don't see anything.

KINGSTON: You are an ass, Kuroma. You lack imagination! What do you think my rivals are doing at this very hour? You certainly know who I mean... the three wogs whose places of birth are not well-known! Plotting for ever, to outmatch me in greatness, rank and glamour of nobility!

KUROMA: Nothing much... their finances are not sound. Their coffers are dry.

KINGSTON: Be vigilant, Kuroma. I distrust those people. Under my very nose, one of them may effect a glorious feat which could make my star set and dethrone me quitely! I have a lot of naira, and my reserve is inexhaustible... So open your eyes, and buy over people if necessary. Make spies of them. I must know all that's happening around me! Am I not the greatest of kings, the Sun-king if you wish? Can a Sun-king have a shady zone, however small, in his kingdom?

KUROMA: (*Who has lost his arrogance*) No, Mr Kingston, he cannot! But must I follow your instructions?

KINGSTON: (*Out of himself*) There are orders, Kuroma, you cannot disregard.

KUROMA: (*Looking like a beaten dog*) Yes, your Majesty, I shall surround myself with spies.

KINGSTON: Faithful spies who, being honest and upright, will not distort the truth!

KUROMA: No, your Majesty!

KINGSTON: Above all, not double agents selling themselves out to the highest bidder!

KUROMA: No, Majesty, I'll be watchful!

KINGSTON: Be vigilant! You have a golden position that you must not lose.

KUROMA: (*Aloud*) I'll be vigilant your Majesty! (*Speaking off*) He's a sick man. Is it necessary for him to own at all costs the most beautiful, the most uncommon and above all the most expensive things? To be precise, this gentleman owns seven cars, the biggest that exist... one for each day of the week. Four Mercedes and three Rollsroyce, just for his personal use! He has thirty-two wives and concubines living in his house. He has thus a woman for each day of the month and he has bought a car for each one of them! Added to the seven monsters, the ambulance, the two forty seater bus-lorries, the four delivery vans, this makes a car park of forty-six vehicles! I am surprised that he has not joined a Hearse to that collection!

Then there are gadgets of the very latest fashion, telephone apparatuses made of solid gold, television sets, videos, intercoms, transmitting radio sets and beds also made of solid gold! Yes, of solid gold! He's a sick man alright! (*aloud*) I will watch out Majesty... I will watch out (*he moves towards the door*).

KINGSTON: (*Aloud*) Good, watch out and keep your eyes open! We'll talk about culture a bit later, after my siesta.

KUROMA: Yes sir... er... yes Majesty (*he goes out*).

KINGSTON: (*Left alone with the servant and walking up and down*) This poor Kuroma is getting old! He cannot follow the rhythm of the present-day life. He is at the age of the telegraph, when he should be at the age of the computer! Soon I may have to replace him. He cannot imagine my needs. I have the greatest need for an aeroplane, and he doesn't realise that! Could he have thought of it? Well, no! I will be the first private individual to own one. Isn't that magnificient? I am only hesitating between a turboprop and a turbojet. Ah! To be the first to fly in his own plane in the whole country! I know many who will have an outburst of jealousy! I'll make the plane twist and turn above the town, even on top of the houses of people I know, to scoff at them! Oh what a pleasure it would be! What infinite joy to be capable of doing what one wants and to get on your neighbours' nerves with impunity! My greatest pleasure is to dazzle and crush! I am the Sun-king and Napoleon combined in one! (*holding his head high, throwing out his chest and making the muscles of his arms protrude*) And by God I shall be successful! (*talking to the servant standing on his right*) What do you think of that, you boor?

THE SERVANT: I think that master is ten times (*thinking deeply*)... that Master is a hundred times... a hundred times? No... I think that Master is a thousand times right! All he has said are correct a thousand times.

KINGSTON: A thousand times? Thousand times only! Fat lump! You are sparing of compliments. You idiot!

THE SERVANT: Sorry Master, a hundred thousand times right!

KINGSTON: That's fine! Well said! Take, this is for your effort! (*giving him two naira*) And remember, with me, be generous with compliments. Add a bit of flattery to your speech and all will go well! And now go

	and seek for my sports adviser who should be waiting in the anteroom, but first of all send the barker to me!
THE SERVANT:	I'll run along, sir...
KINGSTON:	Not sir! Majesty!
THE SERVANT:	Yes your Majesty, sir, er sir Majesty...
KINGSTON:	Imbecile! Moron! How many times must I tell you! What a block head you are! Majesty, your Majesty!... Come on, repeat!
THE SERVANT:	(*Almost in tears*) Majesty, your Majesty, er your Majesty sir... My God, I can't manage...! (*dashing to the door)* I'll call your two men first (*he goes out*).
KINGSTON:	Oh the poor wretch, who cannot call me correctly by my title! He's going to lose his golden position!
THE BARKER:	(*Who from afar makes wild gestures and bows as he approaches*) His most illustrious Majesty, Sun-king and Emperor of all his subjects (*reciting without stopping out of breath)* The ground is a solid element which will not let me bow down any deeper.

KINGSTON: (*In a low voice*) Here is someone who knows how to speak, to place his words and tones wholly at my disposal (*aloud*) Go on my good man. Continue... your words are welcome! If you do the same thing in town, you will have a golden position in my house. Bark at will, my young man, bark!

THE BARKER: In town? I run to the four corners of your estate, bringing to all the subjugated the good word. As a result, your name is at its zenith! They swear by you? All the heroic deeds of your life I proclaim and, when necessary, invent.

KINGSTON: That's marvellous! Sublime! I give you carte blanche, my dear. Invent all you may. Let my name shine forth in history!

THE BARKER: Good Prince, have confidence in me. Hidden in my sleeve are cards and tricks which even the great Turk would envy!

KINGSTON: Barker! Full steam ahead! Bark as much as you can! And you'll have without any doubt all I've promised!

THE BARKER: Till tomorrow my Lord!

KINGSTON: Till tomorrow, yes. But to the plough, set firmly your hand!

THE BARKER:	Not one hand, Majesty. My two hands are firmly set (*going towards the exist*). Regretting only that I don't have three or four to set to the plough! (*he bows and goes out*).
KINGSTON:	(*To the sports adviser who has just entered*) Come on, my good man. Get into the right! I challenge you to a single combat. As such you will see that nothing resists me! (*he moves forward and starts boxing, throwing a straight left to the face of the instructor*).
THE INSTRUCTOR:	(*Who does not falter*) Very good, continue! (*Throwing a straight right to the face of Kingston*). Come on! Parry that one my dear student.
KINGSTON:	(*Who could not parry and is very weakened by the blow he receives*). (*Aloud*) It's not fair play! Stop, I protest! I pay you, don't I, to receive blows and not to give... (*in a low voice*). May the plague put down this dog of an instructor, this stupid ass of an instructor, this hired assassin, this ruffian. Very soon we will see who between the two of us is the boss! (*Aloud*) Let's switch over to something that could enhance my prestige. What do you propose?

THE INSTRUCTOR: (*Hesitating*) Well, I find you a bit too soft for such exercises!

KINGSTON: (*Aloud*) A bit too soft, you mean strong? (*In a low voice*) Such a statement could provoke me to no end.

THE INSTRUCTOR: I said soft. I cannot say strong, when I mean soft!

KINGSTON: My dear sir, if you do not wish to do as I desire, pack up your speeches and outfits. I cannot tolerate such insolence.

THE INSTRUCTOR: But Mr Student, I cannot call you strong, when you are soft!

KINGSTON: Mr Imbecile, know that it's not good to say the truth at all times. Goodbye sir.... Please let me not see you again in this vicinity. I have had enough of your discourtesies and enough of your warblings!

THE INSTRUCTOR: (*Contritely*) But... what? why?

KINGSTON: Stop that useless verbiage! Outside! You have lost the golden position which you've had but which you're unable to keep!

THE INSTRUCTOR: *(Kneeling)* I implore your Majesty. I beg your forgiveness, on my knees. You are hard and strong, oh my Lordship, not soft!

KINGSTON: Well, if you implore me on your knees, and you call me a strong man instead of a soft one, well, everything changes. Even a demon could thus turn himself into an angel.

THE INSTRUCTOR: It is your Lordship who is... a hard angel, but an angel all the same.

KINGSTON: Alright I retain you... and give you another chance. The last! Ah yes, we'll repeat our business tomorrow. See that you have it well in hand!

(*The curtain falls*)

SCENE II

(*Kuroma is in Kingston's main office speaking to a very attractive young lady with a prepossessing face and body*).

KUROMA: (*Speaking to the girl*) My dear Monica, you are going to see an outlandish character. He is not young, he is not handsome. But he is tremendously rich. His immeasurable pride and vanity are at par with his wealth. Monica, if you know how to handle and manoeuvre the fellow, you can make him do all you want. You can hold him by the tip of his nose and make him eat from your hands!

MONICA: But, Uncle Kuroma, I'm afraid of bungling the job, and handling this the wrong way and spoiling the entire show!

KUROMA: My dear Monica, do that for your old uncle! For some time now that animal has been giving me the cold shoulder. I like to be in his high esteem. You know what I mean?

MONICA: What is the freak's name?

KUROMA: Kingston.

MONICA: And in intimacy?

KUROMA: It's for you to device, Monica! Feel free to innovate! He'll be so much impressed if you christen him with a pet name that pleases him!

MONICA: O.K., Uncle Kuroma. I'll do that for you. But I hope this Kingston is not a King Kong!

KUROMA: Not really! His ugliness is not that colossal (*listening*). Here he comes. Hear that noise. That's him. Do wear your most beautiful smile, my darling. Launch your militant charm right from the onset.

KINGSTON: (*Talking to Kuroma right from the door*) Ah you have made a real mess in terms of providing information! I'm the least informed in the whole country! I am completely in the dark! A little nobody without the least calibre speaks of raising a building having 250 outside openings, and all are in rapture over such a project! And till this minute I knew nothing of it (*noticing the presence of Monica).* Oh! O! (*in a low voice)* Oh how much beauty in a single

	person! (*aloud*) To whom do I have the honour of speaking?
KUROMA:	It is Monica my niece, the eldest daughter of my younger brother.
KINGSTON:	(*Staring at her with lustful eyes*) Well...
MONICA:	I came to offer you my services, Mr. Kingston. I'd like so much to be the assistant to my uncle. He is level-headed and mature, and I have the vivacity of youth.
KINGSTON:	Well thoughtout. Welldone. You combine reason with spirit!
MONICA:	With a drop I hope of the little thing that a woman brings.
KINGSTON:	(*Aloud*) Not a drop, but a whole vessel. (*In a low voice*) Oh how beautiful! She would look so becoming in my collection of wives and concubines.
MONICA:	I heard you speaking about the whippersnapper with 250 outside openings.
KINGSTON:	Yes, what about it?

MONICA: I've got in my head a sharp reply to this project – a counter-attack!

KINGSTON: Tell me quickly. I'm dying to know it!

MONICA: You the great Kingston, Kingston the great, must immediately put up a building having as many outer opening-doors, windows and skylights – as there are days in a year! You'll then see whose praises people sing! They'll sing your praises even more, when you top up the edifice with a tower from which you can gaze upon the whole world!

KINGSTON: (*In a low voice*) Ah gaze upon the world with her by my side! Fantastic! Marvellous! She called me Kingston the great! Phenomenal! (*aloud*) Kuroma! It's done. She's got the job as your assistant on a trial basis. Her idea of a building having as many outer openings as days in a year is fantastic! But be careful the roles are not reserved, and that you become the assistant to your niece! (*in a low voice*) Monica! What a pretty name and what a pretty body! Once in my payroll, she can easily turn from an assistant on a trial basis to my mistress and who knows, my wife!

MONICA: (*In a low voice*) You have a foot in the place, my dear. It's left to you to introduce the other foot, then the arms, and, finally, the body as a whole! (*Aloud*) Mr Kingston, thanks for such a quick acceptance of my offer (*in a low voice*). I know what the dirty pig has in mind! He already sees me sprawling on his bed, but he will soon understand that I am not the "pushover" tart he thinks I am! (*aloud*) Thanks a thousand times, Mr Kingston. When can I start working!

KINGSTON: Right now, at this very moment! What am I saying? You've been with us since an hour ago, two hours ago, since the beginning!

(*The curtain falls*)

SCENE III

(Kuroma and her niece are alone on the stage)

KUROMA: *(Talking to Monica)* You have seen Monica. That was love at first sight! In no time you have been able to twist him round your little fingers! Of this hateful satrap, full of haughtiness and pride, having insults ready at the corner of his lips, fangs always out, identifying himself with a lion, you have made a simple doggy!

MONICA: Yes, Uncle Kuroma. I've knocked him out, conquered him, subjugated him. Now I'm going to make sure that this bow-wow remains as meek as a lamb!

KUROMA: Well done, girl! With a few words you have done what I couldn't have in six months. Believe me, I was hanging precariously in the balance. The rowdy fellow was going to sack me any day.

MONICA: That's what I thought too. The man is a monster of pride...

KUROMA: And of arrogance!

MONICA: I'll have to channel his terrible flaws to our common benefit, Uncle Kuroma. Nothing is lost, quite the contrary. His shortcoming, one of the seven deadly sins, will yet be the mainspring of some great benefit for the two of us.

KUROMA: I am sure of that! I can see you catapulted to the highest realm of politics. At the zenith of your career, you will be a Queen, or an Empress.

MONICA: Uncle Kuroma, what're you dreaming about?

KUROMA: It's a dream I've had, and I believe in the efficacy of dreams. Anyhow, you're armed for such accomplishments. I have sized you up, judged you, impartially. Generous nature has granted you master trumps, body and brain, and you must make the most of them.

MONICA: You're flattering me, Uncle Kuroma.

KUROMA: Not at all... One day you'll be an empress, a queen, a potentate.

MONICA: I'm not aspiring to such giddy heights.

KUROMA: You will see! Opportunity makes the thief and of course the female thief. I know that our Kingston has high aims, very high indeed and that he does not skimp on means and that he does not trouble himself with scruples! If you know how to manoeuvre and you know, you will be very very active, at his side, and at the time of his rise, use him as your cat's paw. Then it is he who will be on your side, for you would have taken the helm in your hands. Before everything, don't you forget to reserve a role for me! And a major one!

MONICA: A major role! You aim too high, dear Uncle!

KUROMA: Not at all my child! It was all in my dream, and it was just like a film in black and white!

MONICA: Whatever he does has to be either good or bad. Let's go and see what he's doing.

KUROMA: Keep a close eye on him, for I sense dramatic happenings before long!

MONICA: Let's go and see, my dear Uncle.

(*The curtain falls*)

SCENE IV

Kingston is in his private office, a vast and luxurious room made of tinted panel glass. The arrangement of this office is such that he can see and hear what's happening and what's said in the big office without being seen or heard. He sits enthroned in a big armchair, engaged in discussion with a person in uniform.

In the big office a crowd of men and women, all standing up, wait for their turn to have a discussion with him.

KINGSTON: (*Talking to the person in uniform*) Colonel Manga, I'm going to tell you something ultra-secret that has never been heard of by anybody, but which you are going to hear at this very moment! Then you'll know what's left for you to do, with promptness in action and discretion. Let's start from the beginning. That's it, Colonel Manga! I've reached such a state of satiety in wealth, that now I am completely dissatisfied, even disgusted. Now only power and honour which derives from it interests me. Nothing else can give me greater satisfaction than that. So politics remains my door of exit! Politics, yes! I have therefore, decided to embark upon that vessel, having no richly coloured uniform, nor the least stripe to plan a coup, a *coup d'etat* I mean! Speaking of coups, it is a successful one I want, a glorious feat which will propel me to the highest level from where I may shine like a star! You cannot imagine what it is to have everything and yet to have the impression of having nothing!

The more I have the more I want! I took delivery of my twin-engined jet plane last week, but now it is a four-engined jet that I want and the time is not very far away when I will want a jumbo jet! You may think: "He is contradicting himself, he is rambling! It is not up to thirty seconds ago that he was complaining of being satiated, even disgusted". Well I am not drivelling, but I'm troubled, and confused. In full confusion, I find this desire for power is my exit door and the only one that remains for me. I see the light of the day at the end of a long tunnel, my shadow covering the whole of our dear nation. There's only one step, Colonel Manga, between this armchair in which I sit and the throne to which I aspire! And you are going to help me to cross over that step! (*in a low voice*) Monica whom I sense as being present here, very near to me, is going to help me too! (*aloud*) I have said enough, Colonel Manga. Speak, it is your turn!

COLONEL MANGA: My dear Kingston, you have said enough to be hanged ten times, shot a hundred times, and to wallow the rest of your days in Kirikiri, the maximal prison.

KINGSTON: (*Laughs*) Manga, my dear, I've made you what you are. You owe me all you are!

COLONEL MANGA: Be merry, Kingston, but laugh on the other side of your face (*looking around him in a worried manner*). I see sinister faces in this crowd of people. Were I the ungrateful wretch...

KINGSTON: What are you driving at?

COLONEL MANGA: (*Making the sign to cut his own neck*) I could be...

KINGSTON: Let's stop all this discussion. Only say yes or no to the question I'm going to ask.

COLONEL MANGA: Go on, ask it!

KINGSTON: It is yes or no, nothing else! No way out!?

COLONEL MANGA: Go on!

KINGSTON: Are you ready to follow me in the race to power?

COLONEL MANGA: I'm ready. For both of us, I foresee victory, crowned with glory and honours.

KINGSTON: Then enough talk for today! Come to my house at dawn tomorrow. We shall be all alone (*pointing to the crowd of people with a gesture of the hand*), without all this band of scramps! Of the two-headed being we are forming. I am the superintendent of finance, the naira power, and you are the army, the sabre power!

COLONEL MANGA: (*Shaking hands with him*) Mr. President, the sabre salutes you! (*he moves towards the door*).

KINGSTON: The finance acknowledges your greetings. Mr Field Marshal! As for a title for me, President or Emperor, we'll see in due course!

COLONEL MANGA: See you soon my Emperor (*he goes out*).

KINGSTON: (*Alone*) And now a little thought for Monica who will be by my side as Empress or Lady President!

(*Going out of his office and clapping to call the attention of the assembled people*) Well, ladies and gentlemen, go now and come back tomorrow. I've seen enough of your faces. I have other fish to fry right now (*the two servants standing outside on the right and left of Kingston's office push the people out without further ado, Kuroma and Monica included, who unnoticed in the crowd, were witnessing what was going on*).

THE TWO SERVANTS: Come on! Out! riffraffs, rogues! How dare you bother our master?

KUROMA: Do not touch me. Don't you see who you're dealing with?

MONICA: Keep your paws off, you boors, you ignoramuses! Can't you differentiate a strumpet from a lady?

ONE OF THE TWO SERVANTS: (*Pushing Monica roughly*) Come on, out, strumpet or lady, out!

MONICA: (*Screams*) Kingston! My darling!

KINGSTON: (*Who has heard Monica's voice and rushes forward*) Monica! Monica! My love! (*giving blows to the two servants*) Idiots! How could you treat your

Lady President, your Queen so harshly! It's you who are going to leave this house and immediately. I am kicking you out of here! Both of you. I am driving away dogs like you, incapable of differentiating the wheat from the chaff, a lady from a trollop (*hugging Monica*). Monica my love!

MONICA: (*Responding to his embrace*) O my kingy! My man! *Mon homme!* (*they hug passionately*).

(*The curtain falls*)

SCENE V

Kingston's big sitting room is decorated with the flags of the Kingstonian Empire which has just been founded. Under a canopy with sparkling colours, the thrones of Emperor Kingston the first and of the Empress Monica are side by side. That of the Emperor is in massive teak-wood, inlaid with ivory. That of the Empress is made of ebony-wood, set with emeralds. The two sovereigns have a very dignified air about them, very grave and very majestic. They are looking at the crowd assembled in the large room.

One recognizes, seated down below, Colonel Manga now a Marshal of the Empire. He is strapped up tight in a gleaming uniform covered with numerous decorations. Kuroma is seated near him. He is soberly dressed in a black suit. In front of him a small placard indicates his title: Mr K.K. Kuroma, Minister of the Interior and of Public Revenue.

A military band plays marching tunes.

MARSHAL MANGA: (*Stands up and grabs the microphone someone presents to him. The music stops*) My friends! My comrades! My brothers! On this first day of the year of your dear empire, I am inviting you all to join me, to thank our august and most serene imperial Highness, Kingston the first and his gracious companion, Empress Monica, to have deigned to hold the reins of our dearest homeland.

It's a very difficult task, overwhelming, back breaking, unrewarding. But noble sentiments impel our sovereigns. We thank God to have sent us such leaders! Let's drink a toast to our dear sovereigns. and to our dear country! To our motherland: Hip hip, hurray! Hip hip, hurray! Hip hip, hurray! (*the crowd repeats it in chorus each time*) To our Empress Monica, hip hip, hurray! Hip hip, hurray! Hip, hip, hurray! (*Kingston and Monica, standing up, make signs to the crowd. Kuroma also stands up smiles and thanks the assembly, when suddenly Kingston collapses onto the ground while a red star forms on his chest*).

MONICA: (*Who rushes forward and shouts*) He's dead! They've killed him! (*Holding Kingston's head in her hands and weeping her heart out*): Kingston, my kingy, my man!... My love! I am here.. I will continue your work... I swear...

MARSHAL MANGA: (*Collapses in turn hit by another bullet*) Oh... they have got me, ouch... but why me? (*he looks at Monica questioningly*) We were not expecting... (*he dies*).

KUROMA: (*Rushes forward and cries*) He's dead! They have killed him too! (*Holding the right hand of the dead man in his right hand*) Manga, my old comrade! I will continue your work, I swear... Monica and I will see to the well being of the empire. (*Panic-stricken the crowd rushes towards the exist in a great disorder and in an indescribable tumult. Monica and Kuroma find themselves alone with the two corpses lying at the end of the room*).

KUROMA: Bravo Monica! You are a fantastic actress! The scene of the sobs is tinged with touching realism!

MONICA: And you, you are an excellent planner and organiser! Kingston and Manga eliminated, both of them in a couple of ticks! You should have seen Manga's head when he died! He must have had the surprise of his life... already he was seeing himself as an Emperor, with me on his side

	and in his bed! Now, there's no longer anybody in our way... The assassin has been liquidated too, hasn't he?
KUROMA:	Of course! Yes! Like the murderer of the murderer! (*showing the stretched out bodies)* Look at them there!
MONICA:	So no more fears! In the eyes of the people we are innocent of this slaughter and catapulted to the top of the ladder!
KUROMA:	You'll have to play the part of the weeping widow for some weeks.
MONICA:	From head to toe, all dressed in black. Black fits me quite you know!
KUROMA:	Before becoming the merry widow who can marry whom she wishes!
MONICA:	When I think that this "ugly toad" had faith in my love, and in his power of seduction! How conceited can men be!
KUROMA:	I admit it Monica. About him especially. Conceited he was up to his finger-tips!

MONICA:	The pride of this man was immeasurable! The position of an Emperor did not satisfy him fully. He was aiming still higher! But what could he expect? Is there anything higher than the position of an absolute monarch? If not that of being in paradise or hell! I am sure that once up there, he would demand to be seated at the right hand side of the Lord!
KUROMA:	(*Laughing*) You speak the truth... Monica. His pride will follow him wherever he goes, from hell to purgatory and even to paradise if he does go there one day.
MONICA:	His immoderate pride misled him. We ought to learn a lesson from his life and from his death.
KUROMA:	To be always humble, reserved and respectful...
MONICA:	Avoiding to attract the wrath of the envious.

(*The curtain falls*)

THE LADY INTRODUCER: (*Alone on the scene*) So you have seen the third of these gentlemen (*pointing to the proud man who reappears and salutes*). Pride, believe me is a big drawback that pushes you to commit irreparable acts. No wonder, it's included among the deadly sins! Often accompanied with arrogance and above all ambition! (*she drives him away, pretending to be giving him strokes of her stick*).

KINGSTON: (*Runs away crying*) How dare you beat Kingston the first? Don't you know me any longer? Me, your Emperor! Me, your Father!

(*The curtain falls*)

(END)

www.ingramcontent.com/pod-product-compliance
Lightning Source LLC
Chambersburg PA
CBHW051521230426
43668CB00012B/1696